Ethel Barrymore

AMERICAN WOMEN of ACHIEVEMENT

Ethel Barrymore

ALEX THORLEIFSON

CHELSEA HOUSE PUBLISHERS

NEW YORK · PHILADELPHIA

Chelsea House Publishers
EDITOR-IN-CHIEF Remmel Nunn
MANAGING EDITOR Karyn Gullen Browne
COPY CHIEF Juliann Barbato
PICTURE EDITOR Adrian G. Allen
ART DIRECTOR Maria Epes
DEPUTY COPY CHIEF Mark Rifkin
ASSISTANT ART DIRECTOR Loraine Machlin
MANUFACTURING MANAGER Gerald Levine
SYSTEMS MANAGER Lindsey Ottman
PRODUCTION MANAGER Joseph Romano
PRODUCTION COORDINATOR Marie Claire Cebrián

American Women of Achievement
SENIOR EDITOR Kathy Kuhtz

Staff for ETHEL BARRYMORE
ASSOCIATE EDITOR Ellen Scordato
COPY EDITOR Philip Koslow
EDITORIAL ASSISTANT Leigh Hope Wood
PICTURE RESEARCHER Michèle Brisson
DESIGNER Diana Blume
COVER ILLUSTRATION Vilma Ortiz

First Printing

1 3 5 7 9 8 6 4 2

Library of Congress Cataloging-in-Publication Data

Thorleifson, Alex.
  Ethel Barrymore/by Alex Thorleifson.
    p. cm.—(American women of achievement)
  Bibliography: p.
  Includes index.
  Summary: An illustrated biography of the famous American
actress whose career flourished in the first half of the twentieth
century.
  ISBN 1-55546-640-0
        0-7910-0427-9 (pbk.)
  1. Barrymore, Ethel, 1879–1959—Juvenile literature.
2. Actors—United States—Biography—Juvenile literature.
[1. Barrymore, Ethel, 1879–1959. 2. Actors and actresses.]
I. Title. II. Series.
PN2287.B3T56 1988
792'.028'0924—dc 19   87-36975
[B]   CIP
[92]   AC

CONTENTS

AMERICAN WOMEN OF ACHIEVEMENT

Abigail Adams
women's rights advocate

Jane Addams
social worker

Louisa May Alcott
author

Marian Anderson
singer

Susan B. Anthony
woman suffragist

Ethel Barrymore
actress

Clara Barton
*founder of the American
Red Cross*

Elizabeth Blackwell
physician

Nellie Bly
journalist

Margaret Bourke-White
photographer

Pearl Buck
author

Rachel Carson
biologist and author

Mary Cassatt
artist

Agnes de Mille
choreographer

Emily Dickinson
poet

Isadora Duncan
dancer

Amelia Earhart
aviator

Mary Baker Eddy
*founder of the Christian
Science church*

Betty Friedan
feminist

Althea Gibson
tennis champion

Emma Goldman
political activist

Helen Hayes
actress

Lillian Hellman
playwright

Katharine Hepburn
actress

Karen Horney
psychoanalyst

Anne Hutchinson
religious leader

Mahalia Jackson
gospel singer

Helen Keller
humanitarian

Jeane Kirkpatrick
diplomat

Emma Lazarus
poet

Clare Boothe Luce
author and diplomat

Barbara McClintock
biologist

Margaret Mead
anthropologist

Edna St. Vincent Millay
poet

Julia Morgan
architect

Grandma Moses
painter

Louise Nevelson
sculptor

Sandra Day O'Connor
Supreme Court justice

Georgia O'Keeffe
painter

Eleanor Roosevelt
diplomat and humanitarian

Wilma Rudolph
champion athlete

Florence Sabin
medical researcher

Beverly Sills
opera singer

Gertrude Stein
author

Gloria Steinem
feminist

Harriet Beecher Stowe
author and abolitionist

Mae West
entertainer

Edith Wharton
author

Phillis Wheatley
poet

Babe Didrikson Zaharias
champion athlete

CHELSEA HOUSE PUBLISHERS

"REMEMBER THE LADIES"

M A T I N A S. H O R N E R

Remember the Ladies." That is what Abigail Adams wrote to her husband, John, then a delegate to the Continental Congress, as the Founding Fathers met in Philadelphia to form a new nation in March of 1776. "Be more generous and favorable to them than your ancestors. Do not put such unlimited power in the hands of the Husbands. If particular care and attention is not paid to the Ladies," Abigail Adams warned, "we are determined to foment a Rebellion, and will not hold ourselves bound by any Laws in which we have no voice, or Representation."

The words of Abigail Adams, one of the earliest American advocates of women's rights, were prophetic. Because when we have not "remembered the ladies," they have, by their words and deeds, reminded us so forcefully of the omission that we cannot fail to remember them. For the history of American women is as interesting and varied as the history of our nation as a whole. American women have played an integral part in founding, settling, and building our country. Some we remember as remarkable women who—against great odds—achieved distinction in the public arena: Anne Hutchinson, who in the 17th century became a charismatic religious leader; Phillis Wheatley, an 18th-century black slave who became a poet; Susan B. Anthony, whose name is synonymous with the 19th-century women's rights movement and who led the struggle to enfranchise women; and, in our own century, Amelia Earhart, the first woman to cross the Atlantic Ocean by air.

These extraordinary women certainly merit our admiration, but other women, "common women," many of them all but forgotten, should also be recognized for their contributions to American thought and culture. Women have been community builders; they have founded schools and formed voluntary associations to help those in need; they have assumed the major responsibility for rearing children, passing on from one generation to the next the values that keep a culture alive. These and innumerable other contributions, once ignored, are now being recognized by scholars, students, and the public. It is exciting and gratifying to realize that a part of our history that was hardly acknowledged a few generations ago is now being studied and brought to light.

In recent decades, the field of women's history has grown from obscurity to a politically controversial splinter movement to academic respectability, in many cases mainstreamed into such traditional disciplines as history, economics, and psychology. Scholars of women, both female and male, have organized research centers at such prestigious institutions as Wellesley College, Stanford University, and the University of California. Other notable centers for women's studies are the Center for the American Woman and Politics at the Eagleton Institute of Politics at Rutgers University; the Henry A. Murray Research Center for the Study of Lives, at Radcliffe College; and the Women's Research and Education Institute, the research arm of the Congressional Caucus on Women's Issues. Other scholars and public figures have established archives and libraries, such as the Schlesinger Library on the History of Women in America, at Radcliffe College, and the Sophia Smith Collection, at Smith College, to collect and preserve the written and tangible legacies of women.

From the initial donation of the Women's Rights Collection in 1943, the Schlesinger Library grew to encompass vast collections documenting the manifold accomplishments of American women. Simultaneously, the women's movement in general and the academic discipline of women's studies in particular also began with a narrow definition and gradually expanded their mandate. Early causes such as woman suffrage and social reform, abolition and organized labor were joined by newer concerns such as the history of women in business and the professions and in politics and government; the study of the family; and social issues such as health policy and education.

Women, as historian Arthur M. Schlesinger, jr., once pointed out, "have constituted the most spectacular casualty of traditional history.

INTRODUCTION

They have made up at least half the human race, but you could never tell that by looking at the books historians write." The new breed of historians is remedying that omission. They have written books about immigrant women and about working-class women who struggled for survival in cities and about black women who met the challenges of life in rural areas. They are telling the stories of women who, despite the barriers of tradition and economics, became lawyers and doctors and public figures.

The women's studies movement has also led scholars to question traditional interpretations of their respective disciplines. For example, the study of war has traditionally been an exercise in military and political analysis, an examination of strategies planned and executed by men. But scholars of women's history have pointed out that wars have also been periods of tremendous change and even opportunity for women, because the very absence of men on the home front enabled them to expand their educational, economic, and professional activities and to assume leadership in their homes.

The early scholars of women's history showed a unique brand of courage in choosing to investigate new subjects and take new approaches to old ones. Often, like their subjects, they endured criticism and even ostracism by their academic colleagues. But their efforts have unquestionably been worthwhile, because with the publication of each new study and book another piece of the historical patchwork is sewn into place, revealing an increasingly comprehensive picture of the role of women in our rich and varied history.

Such books on groups of women are essential, but books that focus on the lives of individuals are equally indispensable. Biographies can be inspirational, offering their readers the example of people with vision who have looked outside themselves for their goals and have often struggled against great obstacles to achieve them. Marian Anderson, for instance, had to overcome racial bigotry in order to perfect her art and perform as a concert singer. Isadora Duncan defied the rules of classical dance to find true artistic freedom. Jane Addams had to break down society's notions of the proper role for women in order to create new social institutions, notably the settlement house. All of these women had to come to terms both with themselves and with the world in which they lived. Only then could they move ahead as pioneers in their chosen callings.

Biography can inspire not only by adulation but also by realism. It helps us to see not only the qualities in others that we hope to emulate but also, perhaps, the weaknesses that made them "human." By helping us identify with the subject on a more personal level they help us to feel that we, too, can achieve such goals. We read about Eleanor Roosevelt, for example, who occupied a unique and seemingly enviable position as the wife of the president. Yet we can sympathize with her inner dilemma: an inherently shy woman who had to force herself to live a most public life in order to use her position to benefit others. We may not be able to imagine ourselves having the immense poetic talent of Emily Dickinson, but from her story we can understand the challenges faced by a creative woman who was expected to fulfill many family responsibilities. And though few of us will ever reach the level of athletic accomplishment displayed by Wilma Rudolph or Babe Zaharias, we can still appreciate their spirit, their overwhelming will to excel.

A biography is a multifaceted lens. It is first of all a magnification, the intimate examination of one particular life. But at the same time, it is a wide-angle lens, informing us about the world in which the subject lived. We come away from reading about one life knowing more about the social, political, and economic fabric of the time. It is for this reason, perhaps, that the great New England essayist Ralph Waldo Emerson wrote, in 1841, "There is properly no history: only biography." And it is also why biography, and particularly women's biography, will continue to fascinate writers and readers alike.

Ethel Barrymore

GARRICK THEATRE

WEST 35TH ST. NEAR BROADWAY

CHARLES FROHMAN Presents
HIS NEW STAR

Miss Ethel Barrymore

*in Captain Jinks of
the Horse Marines*

BY CLYDE FITCH

Posters for the 1901 production of Captain Jinks of the Horse Marines
*billed Ethel Barrymore as a star, but the 21-year-old actress had never
before appeared on Broadway in a leading role. She was shaking with
stage fright when she stepped before the footlights on opening night.*

ONE

Opening Night

One evening early in February 1901, Ethel Barrymore stood backstage at the Garrick Theatre in New York City, nearly paralyzed by fear. A mature young woman of 21, she awaited the line that would cue her appearance onstage in her first starring role in a Broadway production. Although her illustrious family was filled with actors and actresses, her background gave her little comfort. She had never been more frightened in her life, for that night the success or failure of the play, *Captain Jinks of the Horse Marines*—and of her own career—rested squarely on her young shoulders.

Later in her life, when Barrymore was known as the First Lady of the American Stage, she could still vividly remember that February evening. She wrote, "On opening night I had for the first time the terrible sense of responsibility which, ever since, has made every first night a kind of a little dying, an agony of terror that never failed to make me terribly sick." Barrymore was never completely able to overcome her first-night jitters.

Her nervousness that first night on Broadway was understandable, however. The appearance of a new leading actress on the New York stage was an important occasion in 1901. Commercial radio, movies, and television had yet to appear, and theater and vaudeville dominated the entertainment world. Members of Barrymore's family had a long tradition of excellence in both fields, and she knew her performance in *Captain Jinks of the Horse Marines* would be carefully appraised in the newspapers the following day.

That evening she was playing the role of Madame Trentoni, a difficult part that called for an actress who could express a wide range of emotion and also sing and dance. She later described it as "very taxing for so young and inexperienced an actress." Barrymore had been amazed when Clyde Fitch, a successful playwright, said he had her in mind for the starring role when he wrote the play. She had been even more surprised when Charles Frohman, the top theatrical producer of the era, gave her the leading part. The great leading ladies of the day, such as Madame Helena Modjeska and Sarah Bernhardt, were mature women, known for their exotic beauty and imposing presence. Barrymore, young, tall, and slender, was a less arresting figure, but her long golden-brown hair, large, expressive eyes, and fine profile were considerable assets.

As Madame Trentoni she piled her hair up in a sophisticated twist and wore an old-fashioned gown with a bustle, a ruffled, floor-length skirt, and a tight, high-collared bodice. The elegant costume made the most of Barrymore's natural charm and grace. But a wave of terror engulfed her when, peeking through the heavy stage curtains, she saw the well-dressed theatergoers heading down the aisle toward their seats. She dreaded the moment when the play would begin and she would hear the line that cued her entrance onstage.

Five weeks earlier she had lived through a similar attack of stage fright when *Captain Jinks of the Horse*

Barrymore (center) scored her first triumph on stage as Madame Trentoni in Captain Jinks. *Her elaborate costumes set off her grace and beauty; the amusing light comedy showcased her easy, natural performance.*

Marines began its scheduled pre-Broadway tryout in Philadelphia. She had grown up in Philadelphia, and friends there had filled her dressing room with flowers. But fear swept over her while she waited for the curtain to rise. Although warm applause greeted her appearance onstage, she was so frightened that she stared at the floor and mumbled her lines so badly that no one could hear them. As she later wrote in her autobiography, *Memories*, someone in the audience shouted, "Speak up, Ethel. All the Barrymores are good actors."

Heartened by this encouragement, she spoke more loudly and her performance improved. Unfortunately, it was too late to please the critics. They unanimously agreed that Ethel Barrymore would never be a star like the rest of her celebrated family. One female reviewer wrote in the *Philadelphia Inquirer*, "If the young lady who played Madame Trentoni had possessed beauty, charm or talent, this play might have been a success."

After reading the unfavorable reviews, Ethel Barrymore went straight to Charles Frohman and begged him to close the show. Frohman, a short, moon-faced man with a genius for the theater, had a well-deserved reputation for producing long-running plays and creating new stars. He had given Ethel her first small part when she was only 15 years old. Since then she had grown from an awkward, self-conscious teenager into a striking young woman. When Charles Frohman looked at Ethel Barrymore he did not see a frightened

girl; he saw a potential star. Despite her pleading he refused to close the show. *Captain Jinks of the Horse Marines* completed its run in Philadelphia and then moved on to New York and the Garrick Theatre.

Barrymore later remembered praying for an earthquake on the night of the New York opening—for anything at all that would keep the audience away. But she realized that the play had been scheduled to run for the next 2 weeks—14 evening shows and 4 matinees—and she would just have to get through them. She swore that after they were done she would retire from the theater forever.

Her knees went weak as she heard the line that meant it was time to take her place onstage. Once again she stared down at the floor as she spoke her first words. But then a completely unexpected feeling of confidence came over her. She later recalled feeling as if all the actors and actresses in her family stood by her side, offering their help and encouragement. Her voice grew stronger as she moved about the set with a grace she had never before displayed onstage. By the end of the first act her self-doubt had vanished. She knew she had found a home in the theater.

As the performance ended, the audience rose to its feet, shouting, "Bravo! Bravo!" and beating the floor with umbrellas and canes. Their tumultuous applause brought Barrymore back to the stage for one curtain call after another. The evening was a triumph. When the curtain finally closed, a crowd of well-wishers surged backstage. Barrymore's father, Maurice, a well-known leading man, pushed his way through the throng and kissed her hands, telling her how wonderful her performance had been. Charles Frohman bubbled with enthusiasm. Clyde Fitch sang her praises to the eager reporters who waited to interview Broadway's newest star. The next day the critics were equally kind. Barrymore would later record that one of them wrote, "Dear Miss Barrymore, New York is at your feet!"

Within weeks, to her embarrassment and astonishment, a Barrymore cult swept the city. Girls began to dress like her, to style their hair the way she did, and to copy her naturally deep speaking voice. A few weeks after her New York debut she had the pleasure of seeing her name in lights for the first time. The marquee of the Garrick Theatre read: CAPTAIN JINKS OF THE HORSE MARINES STARRING ETHEL BARRYMORE. It sig-

naled her arrival as Broadway's newest and youngest star.

The next day she stopped by Charles Frohman's office to thank him for everything he had done to make her a success. But Frohman told her not to thank him. He said she owed her fame to the people of New York who lined up in front of the Garrick Theatre every day to buy tickets to see the show. Thanks to standing-room-only crowds, the play's run was extended for an additional six months.

When the New York season ended, Frohman sent Barrymore on tour with the play. The first stop was Philadelphia, the city of her birth. It was also the city where she had failed so miserably playing Madame Trentoni seven months earlier. On this visit, she had the satisfaction of being a tremendous hit. This success was only the beginning of her renowned career, which would continue on stage and screen for half a century more.

While her parents pursued their career on the theater circuit, Ethel and her brothers grew up in their grandmother's Philadelphia home. A quiet, well-behaved child around adults, Ethel thoroughly enjoyed outdoor adventures and rough-and-tumble brawls with her brothers in the playroom.

Ethel Barrymore was born better life and new oppor-
delphia, Pennsylvania, on ked to the frontier, and
1879, a member of the fou oneers went, troupes of
tion of a celebrated theatr soon followed. These ac-
Her parents, matinee s ses, singers, and dancers per-
Blythe Barrymore and tents, churches, town halls,
Georgiana Emma Drew and even in the open air. A
were busy and success of these theatrical troupes fea-
who left the raising of members from the Drew side of
spring in the capable h s large and talented family.
ana's mother, Louis Nearly all of Mum Mum's children
known to the children and grandchildren were destined for
Ethel, her older bro the theater. Only her eldest daugh-
younger brother, Joh ter, Louisa, never performed, because
their maternal gr health problems prevented her from
brick Philadelphia appearing onstage. She married a Bos-
the city's theater Arch ton banker named Charles Mendum,
Street Theatre, Drew and their daughter, Georgie Mendum,
managed. grew up to become an actress and a
In the year of E United lifelong friend of Ethel's. Louisa Lane
States was stil om the Drew's son, John Drew, Jr., became a
bloody and divi A single well-known leading man. Georgiana
railroad line u with the Drew, nicknamed Georgie, was Mum
great frontier mericans Mum's youngest and favorite daughter.

Georgie grew up to be a lovely, vivacious young woman, and by the age of 20 she was an experienced performer, especially gifted in comedy.

Maurice Blythe Barrymore, Ethel's father, was born Herbert Blythe in India at Fort Agra during the 1847 Indian army mutiny. He was educated in England, and his parents planned for him to enter the civil service. Such a mundane job did not appeal to the adventurous young man, and a chance meeting with the celebrated English actor and touring stock company manager, Charles Vanderhoff, radically changed young Blythe's plans. He took Barrymore as a stage name and spent the next two years touring England as an actor before traveling to America with Vanderhoff's theatrical company. Once there, Vanderhoff went bankrupt, leaving Barrymore stranded in New York City. He survived his first months in America by accepting any acting job he could get, trying not to worry about the future. Eventually he became a member of a regular New York company of actors.

An extremely handsome actor whose dimpled chin and strong profile made him highly attractive to women, Barrymore soon developed a well-deserved reputation as a leading man who enjoyed romantic relationships with each of his leading ladies. Barrymore moved in the same theatrical circles as John Drew, and the two young men were soon acquainted. John introduced his youngest sister, Georgie, to Barrymore, and before long the couple fell in love. Against her mother's objections, Georgie wed Maurice Barrymore on December 31, 1876. Their first son, Lionel, was born on April 28, 1878. Ethel followed the next year, and John was born on February 15, 1882.

The Drew family into which Barrymore married had a 100-year history in the theater that could be traced back to actor William Haycraft Lane, born in 1796 in Kent, England, during the reign of King George III. William Lane died before his 30th birthday, but his daughter, Louisa Lane, was destined for a distinguished stage career. Louisa was born in Lambeth Parish in London, England, in 1820. At just 12 months of age she made her British theatrical debut when she was carried onstage by her mother, Eliza, who was performing in a play with a script that called for a squalling baby.

When Louisa was seven, the recently widowed Eliza emigrated from Great Britain to the United States in search of greater opportunities. Mother and daughter settled in Philadelphia, where Louisa's American debut took place in September 1827 at the Walnut Street Theatre—the same theater where Ethel would appear as Madame Trentoni 74 years later. Eliza Lane remarried, and Louisa's stepfather, John Kinlock, encouraged his new family's work in the theater—especially Louisa's. In her debut, Louisa Lane played the young duke of York in a Junius Brutus Booth production of *Richard III*. Junius Booth, a successful actor, was also part of an eminent theatrical dynasty. His oldest son, Edwin Booth, became a leading actor and a friend of the Drew-

Both Ethel's mother, Georgie Drew Barrymore (standing), and grandmother, Louisa Lane Drew (seated), were accomplished actresses, as was Louisa's mother, Eliza. The Drew family's acting tradition dates back to 1752.

Barrymore clan. His youngest son, actor John Wilkes Booth, became infamous as the man who assassinated President Abraham Lincoln.

Louisa led an adventurous and highly unconventional life, even for a member of the theatrical community. As a traveling performer she lived through a shipwreck, an epidemic of yellow fever that killed her stepfather, and a native uprising on the island of Jamaica. Louisa divorced her first husband, an exceptionally rare occurrence in 19th-century America, outlived her second, and finally married John Drew, a fellow performer.

She was not a beautiful woman, but her arresting, throaty voice and commanding stage presence captivated audiences. Ethel inherited these traits from her. John Drew, Louisa Lane's third husband, was short, rather plump, and unpretentious. The salient characteristics of his appearance—piercing dark eyes, a thrusting jaw, and heavy eyebrows that nearly met over a prominent nose—were passed on to many of his descendants.

In 1853, John and Louisa Drew, in partnership with fellow actor William Wheatley, assumed management of Philadelphia's Arch Street Theatre. Five years later, in 1858, John Drew began an extended period of touring that took him to California, Australia, and England. By 1861, Louisa Drew had assumed sole control of the Arch Street Theatre, making her the first woman to manage a theater in the United States. When John Drew died suddenly in 1862, she continued with her active and successful career as an actress and stage manager. Somehow she also found the time and energy to raise her three grandchildren: Ethel, John, and Lionel.

Louisa Lane Drew had raised her own children according to strict standards and brought up her three grandchildren exactly the same way. She insisted that Ethel and her brothers use proper diction—every spoken word was to be clearly enunciated and carefully chosen according to its exact meaning. Ethel later recalled that any reference to the theater as a "show" brought a derisive sniff and arched eyebrows: "Show . . . do you mean the circus?" Mum Mum would ask. She demanded punctuality at all times, particularly at meals. Proper deportment was also a must. Mum Mum did not tolerate slouching, dirty hands, or uncombed hair in her presence. Any infraction of or deviation from her rules would be met by arched eyebrows and a cold stare—backed by the unspoken threat of dire punishment that, somehow, never materialized. As Ethel grew up, she came to understand that Mum Mum's cold, forbidding stare masked a warm woman with a fine sense of humor who loved all the family and relished her role as its matriarch.

The Arch Street Theatre in Philadelphia, managed by Louisa Drew, was one of the country's foremost theaters. Celebrated for her performances in classic British comedies, Louisa Drew was also a capable businessperson.

In her autobiography, Ethel fondly remembered how the North 12th Street house (one of several in Philadelphia that Mum Mum lived in) seemed to be an enormous structure of spacious rooms and cavernous halls filled with alarming echoes. The dark, formal furniture was typical of the Victorian era. A large table held family pictures and a music box that played "The Carnival of Venice" when Mum Mum wound it. Ethel, who dreamed of becoming a concert pianist, spent many hours at the square Chickering piano in the living room.

The second floor housed an assortment of relatives. There was a big front bedroom where the children's great-grandmother Eliza Kinlock stayed. Another bedroom belonged to Louisa Drew's son, John Drew, who in the years to come would become a second father to the Barrymore children. Other rooms were reserved for Georgie and Maurice Barrymore, for Sidney Drew, and for Adine Stevens.

The size of such a household was not unusual, for many Americans lived in large, extended families at the end of the 19th century, but the Drew clan was far from typical. Despite the Victorian aura of strict morality and the stringent precepts of conduct under which Lionel, Ethel, and John were brought up, their notorious theatrical family broke all the rules of acceptable behavior. Sidney Drew, known to the Barrymore children as Uncle Googan, was the illegitimate son of Louisa Lane Drew. Adine Stevens, known as Aunt Tibby, was grandfather John Drew's illegitimate daughter by an actress who toured with Drew's company in Australia—who happened to be his own wife's half sister, Georgia.

The household's unconventionality did not extend to the children's upbringing. As was the custom in the Victorian era, they were expected to be seen and not heard in the presence of their elders. Few of the Barrymore children's elders, however, were often present. Even their mother seldom saw them, except on Sundays. All three children were naturally quiet, even shy, when around adults—including their parents. Ethel wistfully remembered telling the hurts and fears of her childhood to a series of housekeepers instead of to her mother. Her most vivid childhood memories were of herself and her brothers, Lionel and John, exploring the old house and getting into mischief. She recalled the day John fell out of a tree, cutting his head so badly that it left a lifetime scar. She herself once fell from a third-floor balcony, miraculously sustaining only minor bruises— although she never forgot how scary it felt to have the breath knocked out of her. Her brothers were her closest playmates during her childhood. She had only vague recollections of parental interference in the life they all led.

One favorite memory of Georgie and Maurice Barrymore stayed with her. When Ethel was a lively four year old and Lionel was six, their parents took them on a thrilling trip, leaving infant John at home. Georgie and Maurice Barrymore had signed to tour with Madame Helena Modjeska, a well-known actress who managed her own acting troupe. The Barrymores rode in a carriage to the railroad station, where they boarded Madame Modjeska's private railroad car, a luxurious Pullman that would take them from city to city for the tour, serving as a rolling hotel. Ethel Barrymore wrote fondly in her autobiography of one day in particular when her mother, whom she regarded as the most beautiful person in the world, made her a dress while Lionel sprawled in the aisle drawing pictures of ships and trains.

Although Ethel adored her mother, her father remained a mysterious stranger. Well known in Broadway bars and night spots as a hard-drinking, witty raconteur, he spent little time with his children. Stories of his scandalous exploits circulated among New York actors for years. Barrymore was handsome enough that prominent actresses such as Madame Modjeska clamored to have him join their touring companies. Although he was in demand, many of his fellow performers felt that he never really worked at his craft or lived up to his potential. His disinclination to learn his lines was renowned. Onstage he was prone to produce outrageous ad-libs and blithely leave the other performers to deal with the ensuing chaos as best they could.

While the Barrymore family toured with Madame Modjeska, Georgie Barrymore was converted to Roman Catholicism by the older actress. Georgie promptly baptized her children Lionel and Ethel in her new faith. She neglected to have the infant John Barry-

more baptized a Catholic when they returned to Philadelphia, a lapse Ethel would one day correct.

After the tour ended, Maurice Barrymore came into an inheritance left him by an English aunt. The Barrymores promptly packed and went to England, Maurice's homeland, and spent two years in London. They quickly secured local acting jobs, and their children were consigned to the care of a nurse. Maurice Barrymore spent his fortune lavishly, entertaining prominent socialites and artists, including the writer Oscar Wilde, the actor Herbert Beerbohm Tree, and the painter Lawrence Alma-Tadema, among others. For Ethel, this trip was the beginning of a lifelong fascination with England. When she and her brother Lionel returned to Philadelphia, they greeted Mum Mum with pronounced English accents.

Ethel was a charming, attractive child. As was the fashion, she wore colorful bands across her high forehead and around the long, flowing curls that fell to her shoulders. Her large blue eyes were widely spaced and deep set under dark, arched eyebrows. She had a firm chin and a well-formed mouth. In profile, she resembled her Drew relatives. Everyone commented on what a lovely and well-behaved young girl she was. However, her shyness and excellent manners concealed an adventurous, independent spirit. On her own, away from adults, Ethel delighted in rough-and-tumble brawls on the floor with the family dogs and wrestling matches with her older brother,

Handsome, witty Maurice Barrymore, who changed his name from Herbert Blythe when he took to the stage, wed Georgie Drew on New Year's Eve, 1876. The couple performed together in a number of plays.

Lionel—often fought to a noisy draw.

Ethel Barrymore began her formal education in 1886 just after returning from England. Georgie Barrymore, following her conversion to Catholicism, insisted that all three of the children attend Catholic schools. Not far from Mum Mum's Philadelphia house was the Academy of Notre Dame, a convent school run by an order of Belgian nuns, and Ethel was sent there as a boarder.

In her autobiography Ethel Barrymore fondly recalled the years she spent at the Academy of Notre Dame. In addition to the required classes, she took piano and singing lessons and had special dancing instruction. But the early months, away from her brothers and Mum Mum for the first time, were difficult ones. Her English accent and special music studies made her feel different from the other students, although she soon learned to love the kind and caring nuns. Ethel's musical talent made the piano the focus of her life. Sister Aloysius was her music teacher, and Ethel quickly became her favorite. Ethel never forgot winning a silver medal for playing the piano in a school competition. However, she always claimed she missed the gold medal because the music she chose to perform lacked the required religious theme.

Never a strong student academically, she looked forward to weekends and vacations with particular relish. Life in the North 12th Street house was always unpredictable. If the family finances flourished, there would be lavish entertainment. On very special Saturdays, Mum Mum would take the children to the Arch Street Theatre, where they could occupy the D box, to which only Mum Mum had a key. Imposing Greek pillars graced the front of the building. Inside, the walls were decorated with maroon velvet panels embellished with gold details, and the floor was covered with thick red carpets—a delightful and mysterious place for three inquisitive youngsters. On weekends when Georgie Barrymore performed in nearby New York City, she took the train to Philadelphia to spend Sunday with the children. These were also very special days. Ethel longed to know her mother better and dreamed of being like her—gay, witty, and entertaining.

Summer vacations were always a happy time. One year, Mum Mum and all the members of the family who were not working stayed at a boarding-house at Fort Wadsworth on Staten Island, New York, near the seashore. The children lived and slept out-of-doors much of the time. Ethel, still very much a tomboy, was an excellent swimmer.

Each fall she looked forward to returning to the Academy of Notre Dame. Her admiration and love for the sisters made an indelible impression on her young mind. For a time, she considered becoming a nun, but her piano playing improved every year, and she soon decided to become a concert pianist instead. On the one occasion when she had the opportunity to play for her father, he was overwhelmed by her skill and promised that no expense would be spared in developing her talent. Unfortunately, Maurice Barrymore had the habit of forgetting his promises. He never mentioned the subject again. Young Ethel learned early that she could never depend on her handsome and charming father.

In school, away from her beloved Mum Mum and brothers, Ethel devoted her time and energy to music. A bit of a loner, she also developed a taste for books. She was still shy and suffered terrible stage fright at school recitations when she had to read poetry out loud in front of her classmates. As a child, Ethel gave no thought to becoming an actress. Fortunately, playing the piano did not terrify her the way reciting did.

She was just 13 when the course of her life altered dramatically. In 1892, during an otherwise normal school week, Mum Mum took Ethel out of the convent and sent her to New York to be with her mother. Georgie Barrymore was ill. When Ethel and her mother were reunited, she found that her mother coughed quietly but persistently. The family had decided that mother and daughter were to go to California, believing the warm climate would soon make Georgie Barrymore well. The two would travel by boat to the Isthmus of Panama, cross the isthmus by train, then take another boat north along the coast to Santa Barbara. (The Panama Canal was not completed until 1914.) For an ordinary 13-year-old girl it would have been an exciting and challenging adventure. For a shy and inexperienced convent student the trip loomed as the experience of a lifetime.

Ethel had a glimpse of the seriousness of her mother's illness when Georgie Barrymore said good-bye to her husband. She cried quietly and begged Maurice Barrymore not to forget her, *ever*. Ethel would not recall the significance of those words until after tragedy struck, because she did not know that Georgie had tuberculosis, for which no cure existed in that era.

The journey west proved uneventful. Ethel spent the entire time with her mother, and although she felt shy and reticent with Georgie Barrymore, she got to know her a bit at a time. The one dark cloud over an otherwise pleasant voyage was her mother's cough, which continued to worsen throughout the trip.

Santa Barbara lived up to its reputation for healthful air. The weather was clear and sunny; the town, clean and lovely. Georgie and Ethel were soon comfortable in a rented cottage covered with roses. Madame Modjeska, who then lived in Los Angeles, made the trip to Santa Barbara and renewed her old friendship. Georgie's new doctor was surprised to learn that his patient would be cared for by her 13-year-old daughter. According to him, it was too much responsibility. But all the adult Drews and Barrymores were involved with their own careers. Ethel was the only close family member available.

During the day Georgie's spirits were high. She continued to receive visitors and enjoyed a limited social life. However, at night her cough seemed worse, and Ethel often heard her mother cry-

Ethel, Georgie, Lionel, and John (left to right) sit for a studio photograph in New York City. Although Ethel adored her mother, she was not close to her and later wrote, "I looked at her in worship and in silence."

ing in bed. Georgie continued to lose weight, but she made light of her illness and refused to discuss it with her daughter.

One Sunday morning after taking Georgie her breakfast, Ethel went to mass by herself. As she walked back to the cottage, a breathless and concerned friend rushed up and called to her to hurry home, for Georgie had suffered a hemorrhage from her lungs. Ethel ran through the bright Sunday morning sunshine to the cottage. She found a crowd of people, few of whom she knew, milling around the house and crowding into the tiny parlor. Georgie had suffered a major hemorrhage and had already lapsed into a coma. Ethel later wrote: "She didn't know me. She was thirty-four and a great and gallant lady, my beloved mother whom I hardly knew." Georgie Drew Barrymore never regained consciousness. She died within the hour, leaving her 13-year-old daughter, Ethel, to bear the grown-up burden of getting herself and her mother's body back to the grief-stricken family in Philadelphia, a continent away.

Ethel remained dry eyed while talking to the undertaker and making arrangements for the cross-country trip. She recalled that she did not cry until she began to pack her mother's beautiful clothes—then she began to weep uncontrollably. But she soon stopped her tears, for much remained for her to do. The duties fell heavily on the 13-year-old convent student, but she showed remarkable fortitude for a young woman—especially considering her sheltered upbringing.

In spite of the kindness and help she received from friends and servants in Santa Barbara and Los Angeles, Ethel recalled the period with utter sadness. Ethel's father, Maurice Barrymore, and her uncle Sidney Drew were advised by telegram of Georgie's passing and asked to inform Mum Mum and Ethel's brothers. Ethel had her mother's body prepared by a local mortician and placed in a casket. She used what little money she had on hand to pay outstanding bills and to prepare for the journey home. There was just enough left to pay for her train ticket. The casket was to travel in the baggage car, and Ethel booked a seat in the coach section for herself. The trip to Chicago, where her father was to meet her, took four days and four nights. Ethel spent every hour of that time sitting up. The train had no dining car, and she did not know that the frequent stops for new passengers and freight were an opportunity to get refreshments at station cafés. Friendly passengers finally told the solemn and somewhat dazed young traveler that she could get food if she wanted it.

Maurice Barrymore met Ethel in Chicago, but he was no help to his grief-stricken daughter during the rest of the trip east. She had to make all the travel arrangements for them both and for her mother's casket because Maurice was virtually hysterical over the loss of his wife. He wept inconsolably, helpless with sorrow. Ethel, who had seldom seen her parents together, was astonished by her father's grief.

Mum Mum met the train in New York and finally relieved Ethel of her heavy burden. She deeply mourned her favorite daughter's death but remained composed in public. Ethel apparently inherited her uncommon strength in the face of tragedy from her strong-minded grandmother. Ethel remarked in her autobiography that one lesson Louisa Drew taught her family was that "our deepest feelings are never to be disclosed. They are our own private affairs, never to be paraded in public. Strong emotions—either sad or glad— may be hurled with gusto at an audience, with the footlights in between— and then we are being not ourselves, but an author's invention that we leave at the stage door."

At Mum Mum's request, the funeral was held at St. Stephen's Episcopal Church in Philadelphia. It was July 1893, and Ethel, in her autobiography, recalled thinking, "Next month I'll be fourteen." At the time she felt more like 40.

Louisa Drew took on responsibility for the three Barrymore children when Georgie died in 1893. A strong, determined woman, she faced an increasing number of burdens: Financial problems soon forced her to close the Arch Street Theatre and sell her house.

THREE

End of an Era

Ethel Barrymore and her brothers had no one to turn to but their stalwart grandmother. Louisa Drew did not fail them, taking complete responsibility for the Barrymore children. Maurice could not be counted on to support them or even to keep in contact. His career was faltering, and he was drinking heavily, a problem that would plague him for the rest of his life. His recent shows had done poorly, and his efforts as a playwright had failed. By then the Arch Street Theatre had also fallen on hard times, and Mum Mum was forced to give up her position as its manager.

She sold the Philadelphia house and spent the summer at her usual Staten Island boardinghouse while she prepared to tour in her most famous role, as Mrs. Malaprop in *The Rivals*, a classic written in the 18th century by Richard Sheridan. Louisa Drew decided that Ethel would return to the convent school in Philadelphia in September, and young John Barrymore, now called Jack by the family, would stay with his uncle John Drew in New York. Lionel, who was old enough to begin earning a living, would have to go on tour with Mum Mum and learn the acting trade, even though he had dreamed of being a painter. For the first time Ethel became aware of the family's deteriorating financial situation.

She returned to the convent school that fall, feeling more like an adult than a child. She began to assume responsibility for her two brothers' well-being, a burden she continued to shoulder for several decades. On learning that her brother Jack had never been baptized in the Catholic faith, she arranged to correct the oversight. Ever resourceful, Ethel asked a 12-year-old friend named Sam McGargle to serve as Jack's godfather while she, who had just turned 14, served as his godmother.

Ethel's concern for her siblings never faltered, even though the three Barrymore children would never again live permanently under the same roof.

Back in school, Ethel rededicated her energies to the piano. She studied hard and had begun to recover from the summer's tragedy when a second devastating blow landed. The sister superior called her out of class one day and handed her a newspaper clipping. Ethel's father, Maurice Barrymore, had married again. Less than three months had passed since Georgie Barrymore's untimely death. It was many years before Ethel could forgive her father for what she considered to be the ultimate betrayal. She felt as if she had lost both of her parents.

A third disaster soon added to Ethel's troubles. At the end of the school term in June 1894, Mum Mum sent for her. Ethel was to join Mum Mum on tour in Canada. The Drews and Barrymores never talked about money either when they had it or when they did not. Ethel would one day write, "It is characteristic of my family that we never talked intimately to each other about important things—*never*. Today I think that is rather tragic." Ethel had to face the financial realities of her situation without explanation, consolation, or guidance from any adult. Her mother was dead, and her newly married father was either unable or unwilling to support his children. The family depended entirely on the income they earned from performing onstage. From that point on Ethel would have to contribute to her own upkeep. Her dream of being a concert pianist shattered as she packed her bags to join Mum Mum in Canada.

Ethel would later recall that she began her stage career because she simply did not know any other way to earn a living, for acting was the family's traditional calling. In addition, economic opportunities for women were very limited at the end of the 19th century. Women could teach school, but Ethel's family could not afford to pay for her to get a teaching certificate. Women could be nurses, which required four years of hospital training, or could become "typewriters," as the women who used the newly perfected typewriters were called. They could work for meager hourly wages in the factories and sweatshops that were springing up in all the big cities. In view of the alternatives, it is not surprising that Ethel chose to pursue the craft of acting.

She took a train to Montreal, where Mum Mum and Uncle Sidney were appearing with the celebrated American actor Joseph Jefferson. In her first appearance onstage Ethel played Julia, a small part in *The Rivals*. She had never before considered a career as an actress and was poorly prepared to be a performer. As she later wrote, "Nobody in our family ever taught me anything about acting, except by absorption, but in our family, absorption was a good way to learn." Her only coaching was the command to memorize her lines.

That night, just prior to her 15th birthday, Ethel went before the Montreal audience as Julia. Aunt Gladys, Uncle Sidney's wife, played the part of Lydia Languish. The two of them sat on a sofa facing Mum Mum as Mrs. Malaprop. As Ethel said her first line, she saw Aunt Gladys's face go completely blank—she had forgotten the response to Ethel's line. Ethel felt the sheer terror of stage fright almost overwhelm her, but she recovered enough to speak her own lines as well as the lines Aunt Gladys was supposed to say. She saw Mum Mum lay her fan on her lap and give a little nod of satisfaction. Eventually Gladys recovered, and the play continued with the audience unaware that Ethel had handled her first stage crisis like an experienced performer. It was a real trial for Ethel, but she had survived. She had cleared the first hurdle.

Louisa Drew left the company shortly after Ethel's introduction to acting and returned to New York on "family business." In fact, Ethel's beloved Mum Mum was too old, too tired, and too discouraged by the year's tragic events to go on performing. The company was still managed by Uncle Sidney, who was now also charged with the care of his young niece. Managing the company was becoming a difficult job. When Louisa Drew had played Mrs. Malaprop the theaters had been full. The actress who replaced her was Aunt Gladys's mother, Mrs. McKee Rankin. Although she was a member of another well-known acting family, she did not have Louisa Drew's drawing power, and the company had difficulty paying bills and salaries. In one town the orchestra refused to perform without pay, and Ethel found herself obliged to play the piano between acts to entertain the

audience. She had to race backstage afterward to make her entrance on cue. After a series of financially disastrous one-night shows the company reached St. John, New Brunswick, only to discover they were completely out of funds. Ethel recalled Uncle Sidney telling her to "dress thoroughly" before she left the hotel to go to the theater. Still not familiar with all of the touring company's operations, she did not understand that instruction to dress thoroughly meant that she was to wear as much of her wardrobe as she could get on before leaving the hotel. The company would perform at the theater, collect their pay, and skip town after midnight, leaving their bills unpaid and their remaining belongings at the hotel.

Ethel could not return to Philadelphia, for the house there had been sold. Mum Mum was living in a residential hotel on Broadway, where her son, John Drew, now a successful leading man, leased a suite of rooms. Ethel joined her there and stayed in a tiny, ill-lit room next to her grandmother's. In order to earn an income to pay for her lodgings, Ethel had to find theater work, and so began an arduous search.

The Drew-Barrymore clan faced several radical readjustments. In the past, Mum Mum had been an anchor not only for her Barrymore grandchildren but also for the Drew family. Uncle John Drew assumed that responsibility next, acting as the patriarch who made family decisions and offered help where and when it was needed. John Drew had become one of the most popular actors in the country. He was on the

Louisa Drew played the role of Mrs. Malaprop in The Rivals, *to great acclaim, for 11 years in Philadelphia. She was forced to return to the part and tour throughout eastern Canada, accompanied by Ethel, when she ran out of money to pay for the Barrymore children's schooling.*

brink of taking his place as a great international star.

By 1894 the fundamental structure of the theater business had changed. In the past, individual producers—often actors—had organized and funded plays, conducted tours, seen to their own advertising, and selected a cast. By the last decade of the century, individual producers were being replaced by the Syndicate, an organization that performed all the functions of the old-fashioned producer—but far more efficiently and effectively. Stars ruled the theater. Plays, previously advertised for their content, were now promoted on the basis of the personality of their leading players.

Mum Mum, as the manager of the Arch Street Theatre, had been an early victim of the alterations in the theater trade. She was unwilling to change with the times and too old to start over. Frail, dignified, and 74, she withdrew from the theater to which she had devoted her life. From that point on, she depended on her son, John Drew.

Unlike his mother, John Drew had anticipated the changes taking place in his vocation and capitalized on every possible opportunity. He was one of the first stars the Syndicate created. His agent, Charles Frohman, had an established booking organization, and Drew, already a name in the industry, rocketed to success under Frohman's able guidance.

Ethel Barrymore entered this bewildering arena as a 15-year-old girl with good family connections but limited experience. Mum Mum could no longer provide for the Barrymore children, and John Drew's generosity was all they had left. Lionel, 16 and unwilling to accept acting as his career, entered a series of art schools where his rebellious nature created problems for his teachers. Young Jack spent some time with his father, Maurice Barrymore, who was moderately, if not continuously, successful with his new wife and new career in vaudeville, an enormously popular branch of performing that serious actors spurned as little more than a circus. Jack, after touring with his father, decided he did not want to be an actor. Like Lionel, Jack hoped to make his living as a painter or illustrator. Ethel remained in New York under the watchful and loving eye of Mum Mum.

Facing Mum Mum, however, at the end of a long day and trying to appear unconcerned after repeatedly failing to find work was difficult. Although Ethel faithfully made the rounds of theatrical agencies, she later lamented: "I never did get an engagement in this way, although I went out early in the morning. No smallest chance was offered to me. Not even a stock engagement. Apparently, belonging to a well-known theater family is a handicap rather than a help."

Ethel eventually did get the help she needed from a family friend. Charles Frohman, who had worked with Georgie and Maurice Barrymore in the past, cast John Drew opposite a bright new actress, Maude Adams, in *The Masked Ball*, the English version of a French farce written by a young playwright named Clyde Fitch. *The Masked Ball* made Drew and Adams superstars and raised Frohman to the top echelon of theatrical producers.

It was through John Drew's influence with Frohman that Barrymore landed her first job on the New York stage in *The Bauble Shop*, another Frohman production starring Drew and Adams, supported by Elsie De Wolfe. Barrymore was given a walk-on part (one with no lines). She carried a tea tray onstage but, more important, also served as De Wolfe's understudy. It would be her job to take over the part if illness prevented De Wolfe from performing. At 15, Barrymore was earning $30 a week, which was enough to support herself in those days.

She was soon entirely on her own. John Drew sent his daughter, Louise, to school in France, and Mum Mum went as her chaperon. Ethel moved to Mrs. Wilson's boardinghouse on West 36th Street, where Maude Adams lived with her mother. For nine dollars a week Ethel had a comfortable but small room, use of a washroom down the hall, and three meals a day. Her first cousin Georgie Mendum, who had come from Boston to try her luck on the New York stage, also lived at Mrs. Wilson's, and the two struggling young actresses became good friends.

At the end of the scheduled three-month New York engagement, *The Bauble Shop* was to go on tour. De Wolfe declined to continue with the play, and after several matinee trials, Barrymore was cast in her part, as Lady Kate Fennell. The part required little more than the ability to wear elaborate costumes well, which was fortunate for Barrymore because she still had little solid acting experience. She toured Boston, Philadelphia, St. Louis, and many other American cities. Her poise grew each time the stage curtain rose. In Chicago one critic referred to her in his column as "an opalescent dream named Ethel Barrymore that came on and played Lady Kate." Barrymore was on her way to becoming a lady of the theater.

By 1896 she had become a regular in Frohman's productions, playing bit parts and supporting roles in successful plays featuring John Drew. Barrymore was working steadily, making a decent living, and had developed into a beautiful and graceful young lady. Her entrances onstage were often met by subdued but very evident applause, a tribute not lost on the canny Frohman. Her uncle's prominence and elegant manner made him a popular guest of wealthy, artistic socialites, and Barrymore's looks and charm ensured that she was also in great demand. Although she would have preferred to be known for her acting, Barrymore's name became far more familiar to readers of the society columns than to readers of theater reviews.

As Ethel traveled throughout the United States on tours with various plays in which John Drew starred, she was invited to elegant homes, glittering balls, dinners, teas, and lively cotillions, most of which were written up in the newspapers. The realities of her daily life, however, were not chronicled in the society pages and presented a sharp contrast to the glamorous life that readers supposed she led. Ethel made very little money, stayed in the cheapest lodgings she could find, and had only a few outfits of well-worn but respectable clothes. Her convent education had included sewing instruction, which she put to good use ingeniously trimming, altering, and rearranging her two good dresses for numerous social engagements. Throughout this difficult period, she found some consolation in reading voraciously—especially fiction and poetry—and numbered authors as varied as Mark Twain, Alexandre Dumas, Henry and William James, Walt Whitman, and William Blake among her favorites. Although she knew by then she would never be a concert pianist, her love of music was a solace as well, and she enjoyed attending concerts as much—perhaps more—for the opportunity to hear fine performances as for the chance to mingle with the high society who invited her.

Barrymore met many wealthy Americans who made annual visits to Great Britain and the Continent, and she listened eagerly to their stories. She had never forgotten her trip to London with her parents and longed to return. She saved her money, hoping her career would allow her to vacation there someday. One night, while touring with John Drew in a play entitled *Rosemary*, Uncle John handed her a telegram from Frohman that read: WOULD ETHEL LIKE TO GO TO LONDON WITH GILLETTE IN SECRET SERVICE? William Gillette, a handsome leading man, had for some time been Ethel's idol, and she had nursed a serious adolescent crush on him. She had attended quite a few of his matinee performances of *Secret Service*. The combination of not only going to England but also performing with Gillette proved irresistible. She accepted the offer immediately.

Barrymore's part in *Secret Service* was very small, but once again, she understudied the ingenue, or young female lead, Odette Tyler. When Tyler became ill Barrymore played the lead until a new star was brought in, and according to contemporary accounts she acquitted herself well. Heartbroken at the loss of the larger part, Barrymore returned to her original role. But her increased exposure to British audiences had gained her a few favorable reviews from the critics. At the end of *Secret Service* Barrymore decided to make every effort to remain in England, a country she had come to love. She had met many new friends in London and was soon caught up in a social whirl, just as she had been in the American cities she visited.

Back home Mum Mum had moved to Larchmont, a suburb of New York City, and taken Jack Barrymore with her. She had become quite frail, and young Jack was a kind and considerate companion. Although still in his early teens, he managed to take excellent care of his beloved Mum Mum. Ethel, alarmed

*Ethel carried a tea tray on stage in **Rosemary** but had no lines. Her uncle John Drew, who starred in the production, frequently gave her small parts so she could support herself.*

after hearing of Mum Mum's weakened condition, borrowed money from a well-to-do friend, returned to the United States, and visited Larchmont for a week before rushing back to London. A short time later she was advised by telegram of Louisa Lane Drew's passing—Mum Mum had died quietly in her sleep one night.

This was not the last tragedy in Barrymore's life, but it was among her greatest losses. She slowly assumed the responsibilities that Mum Mum had shouldered. A new era had begun.

Barrymore loved to read and enjoyed books on a wide variety of subjects. Her extensive interests and ready wit helped make her a favorite dinner guest in the highest echelons of society.

FOUR

The Legend Begins

Ethel Barrymore had endured four painful, difficult years after the death of her mother. In 1897 the loss of her beloved Mum Mum added to the young woman's burdens, which included continuing financial insecurity. All three Barrymore children had been left adrift, without a home together or parental supervision. But 18-year-old Ethel Barrymore was an exceptional, courageous girl who had inherited her grandmother's strong will. The Barrymore children, with the aid of family and friends, would survive and flourish.

During those years of loss and mourning, Barrymore discovered two very important facts about herself. First, in spite of being painfully shy, she found that she could meet the demands of both scripts and audiences. The opportunities to watch John Drew and Maude Adams performing, to work with and understudy performers such as De Wolfe, and to actually perform

well in front of the public proved enormously satisfying. She loved touring with the traveling companies, discovering new places and people. She was young, very beautiful, and dignified beyond her years—well equipped to move comfortably in the theatrical circles populated by her relatives and their friends. Being the daughter of Georgie and Maurice Barrymore and the niece of the celebrated John Drew opened many doors. Wherever young Barrymore went she was invited into elevated circles populated by political, religious, and artistic leaders.

In this setting Barrymore discovered her second talent. She found that, despite her reticent nature, she loved meeting interesting new people, and to her delight she was obviously well liked in return. The acquaintances she made in her travels often became her lifelong friends. She was a sparkling conversationalist, for she possessed a lively mind, a wide variety of interests that included sports, literature, and music, and an insatiable desire to learn. As she toured the major cities of America, she studied each one's history. Although she never graduated from high school, she gave herself a thorough education by reading constantly.

If her performances in various supporting roles and bit parts did not merit consistent attention in the theatrical section of the newspapers, her social activities were deemed more than worthy of being chronicled in the gossip columns. Her family background, good looks, charm, and elite acquaintances piqued the interest of the public. In 1896 a society reporter wrote favorably of Ethel, "Her manners are unaffected, and she has a frank unconventionality which is refreshing without being bizarre."

After Mum Mum's death in 1897, Ethel Barrymore's professional and personal life in London took an exciting turn when she joined Sir Henry Irving's theatrical company. Irving was England's most well known actor, as eminent in his day as Sir Laurence Olivier in the 20th century. Irving assigned Barrymore small parts in both *The Belle* and *Peter the Great*. The two plays were presented alternately on succeeding nights in London and then on a tour of the English countryside. Barrymore learned much from observing the seasoned members of the troupe.

As was often the case in her early career, Barrymore's performances in these roles are less well remembered than the romantic entanglement that ensued. The author of *Peter The Great* was Sir Henry's son, Laurence Irving, a serious student of Russian literature. Barrymore often spent afternoons with Laurence and played the piano for him. Viewing him through a haze of romanticism, she delighted in playing melancholy Russian music to suit his brooding silences. She was enthralled with the rather gloomy young man, and soon they were engaged to be married. When Barrymore informed her father, Maurice, of the happy tidings, he cabled back, CONGRATULATIONS LOVE FATHER.

After the engagement announcement, Laurence's spirits rose and he became far more happy and cheerful. Ethel, who had fallen in love with his somber side, promptly canceled the arrangement. When she advised Maurice of the new development, he cabled, CONGRATULATIONS LOVE FATHER.

While Ethel stayed on in England, her brother Jack, by then 15, was sent to England for what Maurice Barrymore called a "proper British education." Jack entered King's College, Wimbledon, where he was mediocre at his studies but immensely successful

For a short time in 1898, Barrymore and Gerald du Maurier planned to marry, but Barrymore broke the engagement. Gerald later married another young woman, had a daughter, and named her Daphne (his nickname for Ethel during their courtship). Daphne du Maurier grew up to become an immensely popular novelist.

at sports, drinking, and flirting with girls. He often skipped school to spend time with friends in London, and by his 16th birthday he was rumored to be having an affair with the young wife of a duke.

Ethel was determined to mend her younger brother's ways. She took him to many parties with her, hoping to involve him with a different social set, but Jack was shy and very quiet among her friends. He did confess to Ethel that he wanted to be an artist, and she persuaded him to enter the Slade School of Arts in London. He stayed in England for another year following Ethel's return to America.

Ethel's busy life in cosmopolitan London soon turned up another ardent admirer, Gerald du Maurier. He was reputed to possess great charm, wit, and gaiety, which went far to compensate for his lack of good looks. Barrymore found her friends' reports accurate, and she felt certain this time she had found the right suitor. When news of the intended marriage was related in 1898 in the *New York Morning Telegraph*, the reporter wrote: "Mr. du Maurier impressed most of those who beheld him as being scarcely ripe. His physique was frail to the point of attenuation, his legs looked for all the world like a couple of sectional gas pipes with abrupt bony projections midway between the floor and their jointure to the trunk. Ethel, in all the radiance of her young loveliness, will be far and away the spectacular feature of the wedding." When du Maurier's mother sat Barrymore down and began giving her instructions on how to dress Gerald in winter and on what foods he could and could not eat, Barrymore, aghast, broke off the engagement and abruptly returned to America.

All of Barrymore's exploits in England, both her acting career and her amorous adventures, had been avidly reported in the American press. Every unsubstantiated rumor and many fictitious interviews, to Barrymore's dismay, appeared in the tabloids and magazines in both England and at home. This free publicity may have been spontaneous, but some was attributable to the efforts of Syndicate promoters. The astute Frohman would never overlook an opportunity to publicize a performer under his management.

Barrymore's return to America introduced her to another round of dedicated suitors. The gossip columns soon reported her engagement to a young socialite, Charles Delevan Witmore, and then to Ernest Lawford, an actor playing the pirate captain opposite Maude Adams in *Peter Pan*. Barrymore deplored these stories. She denied them outright and attributed her exploitation to her familiar family name and the moderate success of her budding career. Often the articles were headlined: ETHEL BARRYMORE—THE MOST ENGAGED GIRL IN AMERICA. The publicity extended across America and also appeared in England—an astonishing amount of attention for a stage personality still in her teens.

As Barrymore matured in the years following her grandmother's death, the acting profession was also developing and changing in style. Throughout the 19th century actors heavily emphasized comic or emotionally charged lines. Older actors were prone to strike exaggerated attitudes as they moved through their parts. Barrymore brought a new naturalness to the stage, a way of delivering an important line quietly, without histrionics. Soon the public demanded more realism onstage and preferred actors who could portray life more plainly. Barrymore had the talent and the ability to satisfy this demand. In her own quiet way she contributed to the growth of the craft of stage acting.

Her own growth as an actress continued. In 1899, Charles Frohman gave Barrymore the demanding part of the 30-year-old Stella de Gex in *His Excellency, the Governor* even though he had declined to cast so young an actress in that role during the play's New York run. Barrymore donned a wig and a low-cut black gown to look more mature and toured with the play for eight weeks of one-night performances. Performing, packing, climbing onto a train and off again for another show—a long string of one-night stands could be a grueling ordeal. Barrymore was then a young woman who had more than enough energy to sustain such a schedule, and she maintained throughout her career that she never minded the effort. She recognized that audiences in towns that host one performance come to the theater for a rare, highly valued chance to see a play, and she noted that "they were so eager to be pleased. . . .

You know they are with you and you don't have that extra drain on your energy to keep them from coughing or moving about in their seats."

The role of Stella de Gex required that Barrymore act a part far older than her years. Although she claimed she learned acting by absorption, her perceptive appraisals of other performers contributed greatly to her developing style. Barrymore noted: "Uncle Jack [John Drew] . . . acted so naturally that he never seemed to be acting, so naturally that he never let anyone see a wheel going around. In *His Excellency* I began to understand the necessity of covering up those wheels, of never letting one of them show, no matter what the critics might say, no matter if some wheely actresses seemed to be successful." Whatever the prevailing opinion of "wheely" actresses was, Barrymore's own light touch found favor with audiences across the country. America was smitten with the glamorous young actress, and the sizzling reports of her romances in the highest social circles on two continents only enhanced the box-office receipts.

Barrymore saved enough money from her weekly salary—now a magnificent $80—in *His Excellency, the Governor* to return to England for the summer, when most theaters were closed, anyway. While there, she stayed with her friend the duchess of Sutherland at her London estate, called Stafford House. From this palatial home Barrymore made her social calls. She attended gala events and met the most distinguished people in England. When the Suther-

Left to right: *Lady Selbie-Bigge, the duchess of York, Lady Oxford, Lady Margot Asquith, and Mrs. Baldwin. Barrymore was well known as a glamour girl who mingled with the highest society and was particularly friendly with Herbert and Margot Asquith. Although she numbered some of the most prominent people in England and America among her friends—and former suitors—she yearned to make her mark on stage rather than in the gossip columns.*

lands left London to return to their castle, Dunrobin, in Scotland, Barrymore went along as an honored house guest. The social season was formally in progress, and Barrymore was one of the most popular visitors from America among the British aristocracy. Barrymore decided that America was where she would work at her trade, but England, with its elegance and tradition, would be reserved for vacations. She vowed to spend each summer there.

She returned to America in the fall of 1900 with two concerns uppermost in her mind. She was upset that each time she met an eligible bachelor, word somehow reached the press that she was engaged. Occasionally, news of engagements to men she had never met appeared in the papers as well. When the rising young politician Winston Churchill, who later became Great Britain's prime minister during World War II, visited Dunrobin, a rumor surfaced almost instantly that the two celebrities were engaged. Barrymore suspected that Frohman was in some way behind this report, among others. She was also increasingly aware that her reputation as a socialite was overshadowing her work in the theater. In England many people said that Barrymore performed as a hobby, that she did it only for her own amusement. American theatrical critics noted that she had never performed the lead in a play, nor had she starred in a longrunning Broadway show. Perhaps, they speculated, she was only a celebrity, not a serious actress. Despite her suspicions about the source of her public-

ity, she turned the problem of obtaining more ambitious roles, including the lead in an important play, over to Frohman, who remained a family friend as well as her manager and producer.

Frohman would never admit to being the source of so much gossip about Barrymore. As her agent and friend, he had faith that she was much more than a celebrity. He had already arranged with Clyde Fitch, America's foremost playwright, to produce a play specifically tailored to Barrymore's unique talents. Neither man discussed the play with her, but both let it be known to the public that *Captain Jinks of the Horse Marines* was being written specifically for Miss Ethel Barrymore.

Captain Jinks was a delightful comic story about Madame Trentoni, a famous European opera star, who comes to America to increase her fortune and fame. In the play, the news of her coming reaches three young officers in the horse marines (as mounted soldiers were then called), who decide to pool their resources in an effort to woo the rich performer. They mistakenly assume that Madame Trentoni is an unattractive older woman whose only charm is her great wealth. The officers plan for the most successful suitor of the three to marry Madame Trentoni, then divide her riches three ways. Captain Jinks, however, falls in love with the young, beautiful, and charming singer and breaks his contract with his friends. True love wins out.

The play and Barrymore were given a lukewarm reception in their Philadelphia tryout, in part because of her paralyzing attack of stage fright. But by the time the production reached Broadway in New York, Barrymore had mastered the part. It became a major hit of the season and played to full houses well into the summer, when Barrymore again escaped to her beloved London for the social season.

While Ethel climbed to stardom, the Barrymore family underwent another series of dramatic readjustments. Maurice Barrymore had claimed he had left the serious theater forever to work on the lowly but lucrative vaudeville circuit. In the autumn of 1900, however, he was persuaded to return for an appearance in *Battle of the Strong*, supporting a well-known actress, Marie Burroughs. Opening in Louisville, Kentucky, in November, the play was a success. But only weeks later, reports reached New York that Barrymore was on the verge of a breakdown. His behavior had become so erratic that his fellow actors complained about having to work with him. Barrymore was subsequently fired from the play, and on his return to New York, friends and family were deeply disturbed by his strange and offensive behavior. He wrote bizarre letters to newspaper editors and created public scenes during which he accused theater managers of being responsible for his failure as an actor and a playwright. He finally returned to vaudeville, where he felt his talents were better appreciated. Ethel had seen little of her father after his remarriage, but the rumors and newspaper reports concerning his behavior

left her painfully aware of his advancing years and deteriorating health.

Maurice Barrymore's brief congratulatory appearance at her opening triumph in *Captain Jinks* was a reassuring moment for Ethel. However, within weeks he suffered a complete mental collapse. The family faced a dreadful decision. Maurice Barrymore could no longer care for himself and would have to be institutionalized. Jack Barrymore, just 19, was given the daunting job of getting his father into care and used a ruse to bring Maurice to Bellevue Hospital. When Maurice recognized the dreaded insane asylum, he commented: "My son has an exaggerated idea about my condition."

Maurice was suffering, according to the doctors, "from absinthe [a potent alcoholic drink] addiction and incipient paresis." His mental and physical condition continued to deteriorate, and he soon reached a homicidal phase. His doctors predicted he would live no longer than six more months.

Ethel's salary had reached $100 a week, and she was quick to step forward to support the cost of her father's medical care. Charles Frohman immediately gave her a substantial increase in pay and advised her that she could draw any amount at any time for extraordinary costs her father might incur. Maurice's condition worsened further, and he was moved to a rest home for mental cases in Amityville, Long Island. Despite his doctor's dire prediction, he survived more than six months, and Ethel bore, without a mur-

mur of complaint, the entire cost of his hospitalization until his death four years later in 1905. She visited him regularly and, after his death, had him buried in the family plot in Philadelphia. It was a sad and lonely ending for the handsome and celebrated Maurice Barrymore.

Captain Jinks of the Horse Marines continued its immensely successful run through 1901 and made Ethel Barrymore a star. It ran for two seasons on Broadway and then toured America. Still, some members of the theatrical press maintained that Barrymore was not a great actress. They wrote that her role as Madame Trentoni lacked depth, that it did not present a serious challenge to the young actress. Worse, they claimed that whatever role she played, Ethel Barrymore was always clearly identifiable as the celebrated glamour girl of two continents. It was said that she had no versatility, although even her harshest critics admitted that she possessed beauty, intelligence, and a charismatic charm that filled every stage she occupied. Still, the theatrical world wanted to know if Ethel Barrymore had staying power. Would she ever scale the dramatic heights, critics wondered, that her grandmother Louisa Drew had?

In her autobiography, Barrymore wrote of a memorable visit with Sir Henry Irving, from whom she had learned much in her earliest career. He had seen the reviews of *Captain Jinks* and said, "And so you are a great star now."

Ethel replied that her stage celebrity seemed fleeting and that the press still considered her to be an untested actress. Sir Henry asked what, exactly, the critics were saying, to which Barrymore responded, "They say that I'm good and that I look right, but that I'm always Ethel Barrymore."

Sir Henry, familiar with the vagaries of criticism and the abilities of a great performer, sternly stated, "See to it that they *never* say anything else." Barrymore put her concerns about the critics aside and went back to work.

Although she was still struggling to be taken seriously onstage, by her early twenties she found herself assuming another role that would prove to be important throughout her adult life. Like her beloved Mum Mum, Barrymore became the rock on which the entire Barrymore family rested. She was never too busy with her own career to ensure that her brothers, Lionel and Jack, had whatever they needed. For the next few years she would care for them like a mother rather than a sister. Finding jobs for two unemployed, high-spirited young men was a rather imposing task, but Barrymore was determined to use all of her considerable resources to succeed.

By 1903, Barrymore's success on Broadway enabled her to rent her own apartment for the first time. Since she was 14, following the death of her mother, Barrymore had lived in boardinghouses, hotels, and the homes of friends. She later wrote, "I remember that I had a wonderful time buying the furniture, especially the piano which was the first of the series of Steinways I have owned and loved."

FIVE

The First Lady of the Theater

In the summer of 1901, between seasons of *Captain Jinks*, Barrymore went to Paris for a brief visit and happened to meet with Charles Frohman, who was also traveling in Europe. Over dessert one evening she asked, "What are you going to do about Lionel?" Lionel's theatrical career had ebbed, and he was playing small parts on remote tours, sometimes with Uncle Sidney Drew and Aunt Gladys's family, the Rankins.

Frohman thought awhile and, without further discussion, said, "I'll put him in *The Second Command*." The play was scheduled to open on Broadway in the fall, starring John Drew, the Barrymores' uncle. Lionel played the role of Lieutenant Baker of the 10th Dragoon Guards, and his performance was neither a disaster nor a huge success. But Ethel was proud of having helped her older brother get his first part in a Broadway play. The next year she negotiated a place for Lionel in

another Frohman production on Broadway starring John Drew, *The Mummy and the Humming Bird*. This time Lionel was cast as an Italian organ grinder, an individual with a heavy accent and prone to melodramatic pronouncements.

Lionel dove into preparation for the part, consulting with friends of Ethel's who were willing to help him out, dining in tiny Italian restaurants to observe the waiters, and making the acquaintance of an organ grinder in New York's Little Italy. His hard work and natural talent created a memorable character and earned him rave reviews.

The *New York Telegraph* headlined its article on the play: STAR'S NEPHEW SURPRISES FASHIONABLE EMPIRE AUDIENCE BY HIS CLEVER WORK IN "THE MUMMY AND THE HUMMING BIRD." Lionel next played a commandant in the Boer army in *The Best of Friends*. An important part in a smash hit, *The Other Girl*, followed,

53

and once again his thorough research paid off. In the play his character was a gentle parody of Kid McCoy, a prominent fighter, and Lionel promptly set to work training in McCoy's gym. He and McCoy became friends, and Lionel's perceptive observation of McCoy's and other fighters' idiosyncrasies helped make his character in *The Other Girl* an audience favorite. One critic called him "one of the greatest American character actors." Ironically, the critics recognized Lionel Barrymore as a theatrical genius long before they gave the same praise to his equally talented sister.

Ethel did not neglect her younger brother either. When *Captain Jinks* had finished playing throughout the country, the tour closed in Philadelphia. A bit player left the company, and Ethel assured Frohman that Jack could fill the minor role of a lieutenant in the horse marines. After agreeing, Frohman made the two-hour trip from New York to see if the third Barrymore had the same stage potential as his siblings. Frohman must have been impressed because the next year, 1903, Jack Barrymore opened in Chicago as Max, a role Lionel had played some years before, in Frohman's production of

In 1912, Ethel performed with her brother John on Broadway in a short play called A Slice of Life, *by James Matthew Barrie, author of the children's classic* Peter Pan. *Once established as a Broadway star, Barrymore did all she could to ensure that her brothers were employed as well.*

Magda. The only review of the play, written by the renowned critic Amy Leslie, stated, in part: "The role of Max was essayed by a young actor who calls himself Mr. John Barrymore. He walked about the stage as if he had been all dressed up and forgotten."

Jack Barrymore soon left the play and, with a $50 loan from his ever-patient sister, returned to New York. There he acted in a Clyde Fitch comedy, *Glad of It*. The critics were kinder to Jack Barrymore but treated the play harshly. One reviewer claimed, "The last of the Barrymores, Young Jack, made a successful debut as a press agent, but 'Glad of It' is no more than a half baked success." His promising performance earned him an invitation to tour with William Collier, a well-regarded comedian, in *The Dictator*, which ran for a year and a half and allowed Jack plenty of time to develop his gift as a comic actor. By the early 1900s, Ethel could rest assured that all three Barrymores were making a comfortable living onstage.

Ethel's concern extended beyond her brothers to her employees, friends, and co-workers. Mrs. Wilson, in whose boardinghouse Ethel had stayed in her early years in New York, was hired to make Ethel's dresses in *Captain Jinks*. A former office boy for Frohman was the company manager during that tour and spent 20 years—the rest of his life—working with Barrymore in various capacities. Cousin Georgie Mendum was Barrymore's frequent and lifelong companion, and one maid who traveled to England with Barrymore

during the summer of 1902 stayed in her service for two decades. In her autobiography Barrymore claimed, "I always tried to keep the same people around me if I could, and we were always a happy lot of people."

In 1903, Frohman cast Barrymore in a double bill made up of a short opening play, *Carrots*, followed by the main feature, *A Country Mouse*. Like many Broadway plays in the early 20th century, *A Country Mouse* had been first performed one year earlier in London. Barrymore saw it there during a summer visit, which helped her prepare to play her role when the American dramatic season opened in New York in the autumn. She also took the opportunity while in London to have costumes made for her character. During that era young actors just beginning in the theater had to pay for their costumes, whereas the producer was often willing to buy outfits for his stars. As Barrymore ironically noted, poor young actors had to pay to appear; once they were established—and wealthier—their employer took care of their needs. After Barrymore's triumph in 1901, she no longer gave a thought to paying for her costumes, for her salary kept pace with her popularity. Her concern about her reputation among serious critics still remained.

Barrymore scored another success with the theatergoing public in *Carrots*, in which she played a young French boy, and *A Country Mouse*. One admiring reviewer wrote: "Miss Barrymore as a star is no longer an experiment. Her success in the double bill has established her versatility." The press in general, however, would not let her forget that they still thought of her as more of a celebrity than a serious actress. One columnist, in commenting on a typical Barrymore audience, wrote, "All this week the Savoy Theatre has had the aspect of a Fifth Avenue drawing room." Some were unwilling to take her performances seriously when the theater's best seats were occupied by her high-society friends.

Barrymore followed her appearance in *Carrots* and *The Country Mouse* by another summer visit to London and a return to New York to star in *Cousin Kate*, a play written expressly for her, which then went on a tour of other American cities. When it closed in the spring of 1903, she prepared to return to London. Her life had fallen into a fairly stable pattern, and at last she rented an apartment, on Park Avenue and 40th Street, where she housed a fine grand piano—along with Lionel and Jack occasionally—and a profusion of books, sheet music, and framed prints.

The summer of 1903 was particularly delightful for Ethel Barrymore. She spent it in England, where the nobility continued to treat her as one of their own. She attended a celebrated fancy-dress ball given by the duchess of Devonshire, met the Prince of Wales at another party, and became engaged to charming Harry Graham, a captain in the Coldstream Guards. Barrymore's friends all thought that this time the oft-engaged Barrymore had made a good

match. She had, however, an unfortunate reputation for spending large amounts of money, living and traveling very well, and giving extravagant handouts to her brothers as well as supporting her father. When a friend of Ethel's was asked how Harry Graham could support Barrymore on a captain's low pay, he replied, "Don't worry, Lionel and Jack will support them on the money Ethel gives to Lionel and Jack."

Barrymore loved being in Harry Graham's company. She adored his wit and good humor, but she eventually realized that she did not adore him absolutely. She later wrote: "I might have hurt him if I married him—I will always be glad that we remained friends." She seemed to be having trouble committing herself to anyone as deeply as she was committed to her family.

In 1905 her annual fall return to New York brought a costarring role in *Sunday*, a play set in the old West. Critics carped about the quality of the script, written by four actors, because theater journalists took a rather dim view of performers' writing abilities. Barrymore evinced some of the wit that made her such a popular guest when she remarked that she wondered what the public would say about a play written by four critics. The role did provide her with her first opportunity to play a major character part, someone totally unlike herself. The play, withstanding the critics' barbs, became another huge hit, and Barrymore would later recall that it was while appearing in this particular play that she finally realized that the stage was where she belonged—that it would be her life. She also ad-libbed two lines just before exiting at the end of the second act: "That's all there is. There isn't any more." To Barrymore's astonishment, the phrase became one of the most ubiquitous clichés of the first decades of the 20th century. Even Barrymore admitted: "For some reason that line has been given an importance far beyond its merit or meaning. . . . It meant nothing; it had nothing to do with anything." Nevertheless, it was repeated constantly, and imitators and comedians used it to parody Barrymore throughout her career.

Barrymore remained as concerned with her brothers' success onstage as she was with her own. She impressed on Frohman that both Lionel and Jack could do parts in *Pantaloon*, the first half of her next season's two-play bill, and that Jack could fill a role in the second play, called *Alice-Sit-by-the-Fire*, in which she was to star. Frohman, by then the manager-producer of 15 plays currently touring America, 12 in England, and several more in Europe, would one day be credited with a phenomenal talent for discovering star quality in budding actors, in part because of the help he gave the three Barrymores.

Lionel had been far more upset by the death of his father in 1905 than he realized, and by 1906 he suffered terrible stage fright throughout his appearance in *Pantaloon*. Tormented by fear that he would forget his lines (in fact, he never did) he took a sabbatical from the stage that year to study painting. Ethel, ever generous, was ready with a check to support him and even figured out a way to establish him and his wife in Paris. Lionel's ties to the theater were strong, however. His wife Doris came from a family as steeped in theater history as his own, for she was a daughter of McKee Rankin's, as was Gladys Rankin, old Uncle Sidney Drew's wife.

As the first decade of the 20th century drew to a close, Ethel continued to enjoy great success at the box office. Her name on a theater marquee was a guarantee of a play's financial success. But the press continued to complain that she appeared in trivial plays. Some derided her fans, claiming they were more interested in Barrymore's clothes, her latest social adventures, and whom she dated than in her acting or in the quality of the play. Society reporters did not help matters by continuing to refer to her as America's most engaged woman. But in 1908 that changed.

One bright September day Barrymore was in New York to rehearse a new play called *Lady Frederick*, by Somerset Maugham, an English dramatist and novelist who was enjoying his first taste of literary fame. During lunch with John Drew, his wife, and a few friends who were all planning to spend the weekend at the Drews' fashionable East Hampton, Long Island, home, a tall, handsome young man named Russell Colt stepped through the restaurant door. Drew, who knew Colt, called him over to the table and soon learned that Colt was also spending the weekend in East Hampton. They all took the same train, and as Ethel later wrote, "after that, well, it just happened."

Russell Colt, at 26, was 3 years Ethel's junior and the son of Colonel Samuel P. Colt, the millionaire president of the Industrial Trust Company of Providence, Rhode Island. (The colonel's uncle had invented the Colt revolver.) Russell Colt was well educated, charming, and very spoiled. In March 1909 he and Barrymore announced their engagement, and in short order Barrymore received an invitation to lunch from Colonel Colt.

The meeting proved to be an uncomfortable one. The stock market had recently suffered a downturn, and the Colt family had experienced a financial setback. Colt, overstating the matter slightly, said, "I can't understand why you would want to marry my son. I have no money." She replied that she was not expecting to marry into a fortune and said, "I make enough money for the two of us."

"And how much is that?" Colonel Colt came quickly to the point.

"About $100,000 a year," she replied, adding, "but I think it would be a good thing if Russell had some sort of a job." Russell Colt, who had never worked a day in his life, joined H. L. Horten, a Wall Street brokerage backed by his father. The responsibilities of his new job and impending marriage by no means imbued the young man with a desire for hard work. When asked what train he took to the city, Colt took great pleasure in replying, "I usually *miss* the 10:37."

Because Colt was a Protestant, Barrymore needed the Roman Catholic church's permission to marry him. Bishop O'Connell of Boston, a personal friend of the Barrymores, granted that and added another dispensation that allowed the couple to marry during Lent. They were wed on Sunday, March 14, 1909, with only two witnesses present in a private ceremony kept secret from the press. In attendance were Jack Barrymore and Roswell Colt, Russell's brother. Barrymore planned a working honeymoon. The newlyweds would soon leave on tour with *Lady Frederick*, sharing a private railway car, a wedding present from Colonel Colt.

In June 1909, Charles Frohman announced that henceforth Barrymore would perform only in dramatic roles. He planned to present her, in the future, as a serious actress. But Barrymore's first pregnancy forced Frohman to postpone the opening of *Mid-Channel*, a work by the respected British playwright Arthur Pinero. Frohman was willing to wait, for the play had a truly dramatic role tailor-made for Barrymore. She and her husband summered in Greenwich, Connecticut, and delayed the play until the following winter. In the fall, Ethel and Russell Colt rented a town house on New York's 34th Street, where their first son, Samuel, was born on November 28, 1909. Bedside pictures of Ethel Barrymore Colt, wearing a charming nightdress and lace cap and reclining in bed cuddling little Sam, appeared widely in the newspapers and periodicals of two continents. Barrymore's adoring public

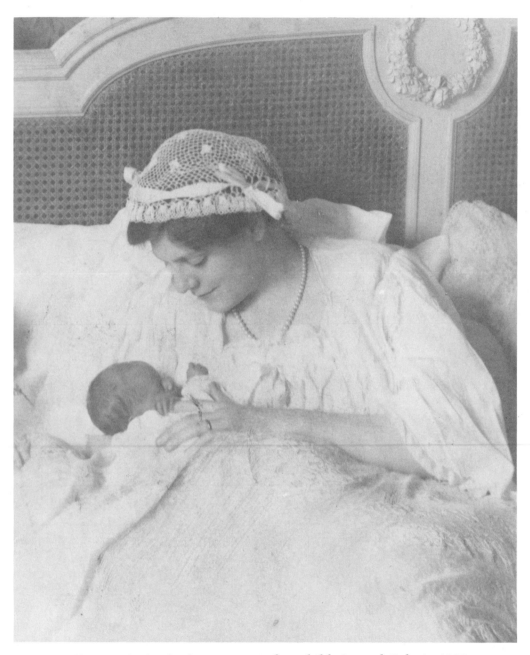

Following the birth of Barrymore's first child, Samuel Colt, in 1909, her fans clamored for details about her new domestic life. Barrymore said of this widely published photograph, "That picture went all over the world; I received copies of it from China, Japan and India."

was treated to an intimate glimpse of the actress's private life. She would later recall unhappily that she was always being written about and photographed. "The goldfish bowl has been one of the hardest things I have had to cope with. Nowadays, there are paid publicists; I would gladly have paid *not* to be written about."

Colonel Colt had apparently recovered from his brief financial problems because, as Ethel Barrymore wrote in her autobiography, when she mentioned that the family would do better living in the country, Russell's father said, "You find a place and I'll give it to you." She and her husband searched all summer and found a 10-acre plot with an old house in Mamaroneck, a small town north of New York City, that suited their needs. It was 20 miles from downtown New York, a considerable commute in those days, but Barrymore loved it. The colonel agreed that it would be a good buy. Unfortunately, Russell Colt detested the house. Nevertheless, Colonel Colt bought it for his son and daughter-in-law, and it became the family's focal point for the rest of Barrymore's life, much as Mum Mum's Philadelphia home had been the cornerstone of the Drew-Barrymore family before the turn of the century.

The role of homemaker and mother was a novel one for Barrymore, but it made superb copy for the newspapers and magazines throughout the nation and in England. The bulk of the articles was devoted to speculation concerning her ability to make two careers succeed—and whether she could domesticate her husband, who had a reputation for chasing women.

It soon became apparent to Barrymore that Russell Colt had very little interest in the theater or in her career. Colt was bored by theatrical people and made no effort to broaden his acquaintances within his wife's circle of friends. Colt, who had been raised among the idle rich, seemed content to let his wife support the family. Colonel Colt, deeply disappointed with his son's irresponsible attitude, refused further financial help. Even so, Russell Colt's casual attitude toward gainful employment did not improve. These rocky moments in the Colts' marriage could be kept from the public—but only for a short while.

Barrymore was anxious to return to work following the birth of her son, for the sake of both her career and the family finances. *Mid-Channel* had opened in London the previous fall with a British actress playing the lead, and the production had failed miserably. Frohman reported this to Barrymore, but she had studied the script and fallen in love with the character she would play: Zoe Blundell, an unhappily married 37-year-old Englishwoman. The Blundells are extremely wealthy and completely incompatible. The script portrays them as a wretched couple, nagging each other continually, each seeking a reason to leave the other. Zoe Blundell, after taking a lover, leaps from a balcony to end her misery. It was a far more serious and demanding role than any Barrymore had played so far, and she clearly recognized the parallels to her own personal life.

She started rehearsals just three weeks after Sam Colt's birth, and *Mid-Channel* opened in February 1910 for a five-week tryout run. Barrymore's performance as Zoe Blundell quieted those who complained about her dramatic capabilities. After the premiere performance in New York's Empire Theatre, Barrymore was again the talk of the theatrical world. One critic wrote that her sparkle and charm were "combined with a nervous intensity, a fire and pathos, which, though it may have been latent, has not been called forth before. She takes a new place on a stage she has long adorned."

The press, however, was reluctant to give Ethel a perfect score. Another critic, in referring to her postnatal weight gain, remarked: "Width has set in—in unexpected places. We now get a somewhat heavy woman who can act considerably, shed damp tears, and suggest dry ones." Other critics proclaimed that, in her new roundness, "she was in her fullest bloom."

Mid-Channel was on tour in New Orleans in November 1910 when the first public reports of marital discord appeared, although Barrymore denied them all. The following July she was doing a repertory tour, playing *Alice-Sit-by-the Fire* and a new short play entitled *The Twelve Pound Look*. On alternate nights she performed in *Mid-Channel* and *Trelawney of the Wells*. The strain of performance was exacerbated by reports in the press that she had visited a lawyer and a notary for the purpose of beginning an action for divorce. Russell Colt, according to hearsay, was having extramarital affairs, and it was remarked that the Colts' marriage had begun to resemble closely that of the Blundells in *Mid-Channel*. Despite the scandal, by the end of the summer the Colts were back at Mamaroneck, and each made public statements denying the gossip and suggesting that Frohman's press agents were again busily stoking the rumor mills. The birth of Ethel Barrymore Colt in 1912 and of John Colt in 1913 helped quash stories of marital strife. The three children were nicknamed Sammy, Sister, and Jackie.

Barrymore always assumed that a theater career and motherhood were perfectly compatible. Although few married women worked outside the home in the first half of the 20th century, Barrymore was descended from three generations of working mothers, and her female forebears were impressive role models. Often asked how she managed to combine work and child rearing, she always dryly replied, "I was born and so, I've always understood, was my mother."

Despite Barrymore's determination to make her marriage work, in the years to come it would become obvious that the Colts enjoyed few periods of extended tranquillity. As an adult,

Barrymore and her costar Charles Dalton appear in Mid-Channel. *She took on the demanding dramatic lead role of Zoe Blundell three weeks after the birth of Sammy.*

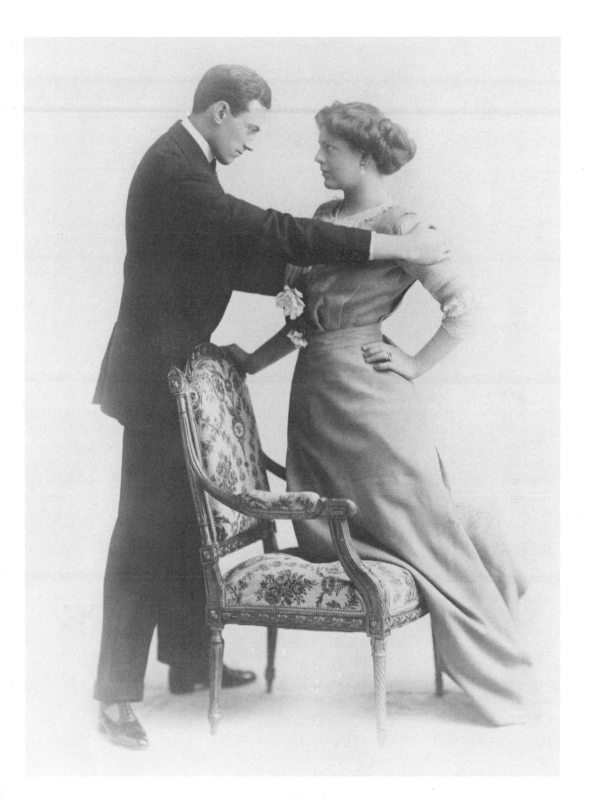

*Ethel with her children, clockwise from upper right: John Drew Colt
(Jackie), Ethel Barrymore Colt (Sister), and Samuel Colt (Sammy).
Russell Colt's unwillingness to work forced Barrymore to stay steadily
employed to support their growing family.*

Ethel Colt Miglietta said in an interview: "Between my mother and father there was absolute incompatibility. It was the most terrible life in the world for a man. On the other side, he did not behave well and was the kind of Palm Beach person my mother, ordinarily, would have found hard to bear. . . . When she found the marriage wasn't working, she was miserable."

When asked to comment on Barrymore as a mother, Miglietta responded:

"Her relations with us were extraordinary in spite of the fact that we were put under the care of governesses and were sent to boarding schools because she was away a good deal of the time. We would see her, after babyhood, at the Ritz in Boston, in Chicago at Christmas, Atlantic City at Easter. We weren't over-mothered by any means. She was a goddess to us. She was wonderful and warm, but let's face it, she did not change our pants."

In 1911, Barrymore starred in the first production of **The Twelve Pound Look**. *The one-act play was a great success, and Barrymore continued to revive it throughout the next 25 years—usually when her money ran short.*

S I X

New Realms to Conquer

Soon after her daughter's birth on April 30, 1913, Barrymore faced a crisis in her professional life as well as in her marriage. During the preceding year, her manager, Charles Frohman, had given several leading roles, particularly suited to Barrymore's talents, to a number of other stars in his stable. He had done so not only because of Barrymore's pregnancy but also because by then he counted a substantial number of other glamorous and talented performers, such as Hattie Williams and Alla Nazimova, among his clients. *Variety* (the newspaper of the entertainment business) reported that Barrymore had considered defecting to Frohman's rivals, the well-known Shubert brothers, Lee and Jacob J. In the tightly knit world of Broadway this would have created an uproar, but it did not come to pass.

Instead, Barrymore told the press that because Frohman had neglected to pro-

vide her with a suitable stage role for the fall Broadway season, she had decided to take *The Twelve Pound Look* on a tour of the vaudeville circuit. This one-act British play, written by James Barrie, the author of *Peter Pan* and a friend of Barrymore's from her days as the darling of London society, had been hugely successful as one part of various double bills. Barrymore thought it would work well in a vaudeville show, which typically featured actors performing celebrated soliloquies, and jugglers, clowns, musicians, magicians, and other entertainers. She also knew the pay was high. Her independent move, in an era when even the most eminent and successful actresses relied on their male producers to make business decisions, startled the theatrical world. She selected a first-rate cast and touring company, including several old friends, supervised rehearsals herself, and took *The Twelve Pound Look* on the road. On her western tour of the Orpheum Theater circuit she twice broke attendance records at the well-known Palace Theater in San Francisco and each week received an immensely satisfying $3,000 paycheck. The schedule was somewhat flexible, and the role was an excellent vehicle for Barrymore's talents.

The Twelve Pound Look is a delightful play. In it Barrymore portrayed a divorced woman who supports herself by working as a secretary. Her ex-husband in the script is selfish and dictatorial, but he has always provided security. When Barrymore's character divorces him, she sacrifices that security but gains self-confidence when she realizes that she can always earn 12 pounds (pounds are units of English currency) a week by typing, so long as she has the proper look or appearance. The play reflected the growing economic emancipation of women of the era as well as Barrymore's financial independence from her husband.

Barrymore eventually overcame Frohman's objections to touring in vaudeville and continued to present *The Twelve Pound Look* during financial crises through the birth of her third child. In subsequent years she returned to the vaudeville circuit time and time again when nothing was available on the Broadway stage and her growing responsibilities demanded additional income. She later wrote of telling a friend, referring to that period when she was having the children, "I kept on working. I *had* to work."

"But why?" the friend asked.

Barrymore's answer was simple, direct, and truthful: "Dough."

Having triumphed in vaudeville, Barrymore turned to the budding movie industry during this period to test her talent. Like vaudeville, motion pictures were considered a second-rate arena for stage actors. Movies were relatively new, still experimental, not very professional, and lacked both sound and color. They were also like vaudeville in being a ready source of income, and some studios paid stage personalities very well, seeking to add a more respectable cachet to the ventures. Barrymore needed money, and she had observed that her older brother had been well rewarded for making the leap to motion pictures.

Lionel and Doris Barrymore had returned from Paris in 1909, when Ethel married. Lionel traveled the vaudeville circuit with Uncle Sidney, Aunt Gladys, and McKee Rankin and then took a job with the pioneering film director D. W. Griffith, whose studio was at 11 East 14th Street in New York. When Griffith went to California, where the light was better and space was cheap, Lionel followed. He played a wide variety of character parts for a salary of $125 per week and wrote scripts as well.

The All Star Feature Corporation enticed Ethel Barrymore with much more than $125 per week. They offered her $15,000 for two weeks' work to do a film called *The Nightingale*, written for her by her late father's close friend Augustus Thomas. One woman critic wrote of the movie: "Girls, we're sure moving pictures are all right now, aren't we? Nothing lowbrow about them if Miss Barrymore loves them, is there? Our taste is vindicated!" Barrymore loved neither the picture nor the reviews, however, although the photoplay was profitable.

Once Barrymore had proved that she could survive without Frohman, they resolved their differences. Two weeks after giving birth to Jackie, her last child, she was hard at work again, rehearsing *Tante*, a work by Haddon Chambers based on a popular novel about an aging, eccentric concert pianist. The play received rave reviews in New York and Washington. One journalist wrote that Barrymore had done "some of the best work of her career." To her surprise and pleasure, the critics who had called her a one-dimensional actress now referred to her as "the first actress of our stage." As she approached her 40th birthday, her once-slim figure had thickened and her lovely face had aged, but her talent had matured.

After *Tante*, Barrymore returned to the Empire Theatre to star with John Drew in *A Scrap of Paper*. Eighteen years had passed since they had last appeared together, and Barrymore was struck anew with admiration for her uncle's work. She later observed, "John Drew's acting was so perfectly effortless that it didn't seem to be acting. Some people used to say, without realizing what a tribute they were paying him, that he only played himself, that he didn't act but just behaved." Drew's own pride in his niece was particularly evident during their curtain calls, as he beamed and presented her to the audience.

John Drew helped Barrymore with more than acting. Polite observers had begun referring to her figure as matronly; other commentators were less delicate. Stung by these remarks, Barrymore used her uncle's weight-reducing program to lose 75 pounds during the summer of 1914. When asked what the very effective program was, she succinctly replied, *"Not eating."*

Although her marriage was still deeply troubled, she spent much time in Mamaroneck with her children. Colonel Colt adored his grandchildren and often invited them to his home in Bristol, Rhode Island, and to his nearby farm. In her autobiography, Barrymore remembered that she and her husband shared one interest, at least. She wrote, "We had a strong bond in our common love of sports." The Colts attended numerous baseball games, including World Series games at the Polo Grounds and Yankee Stadium, polo matches in Westbury, Long Island, tennis games at Forest Hills, and boxing matches at Madison Square Garden. Barrymore particularly appreciated boxing and baseball and collected autographed pictures of well-known prizefighters. The Colts also enjoyed playing poker with friends regularly.

Overleaf: *Critics praised Barrymore's portrayal of an eccentric, difficult concert pianist in* Tante. *She appeared in a number of hits throughout the 1910s and 1920s.*

Such a life required a steady income, and in 1915, Metro Pictures Corporation (which became Metro-Goldwyn-Mayer 9 years later) offered Barrymore $60,000 a year to star in 5 films in the next 2 years. The salary overcame any lingering aversion she had toward movies after *The Nightingale*, and she particularly praised the way one picture titled *The Awakening of Helena Ritchie* turned out.

Several members of the versatile Drew-Barrymore clan moved smoothly before the cameras. In 1914, Jack Barrymore, who had made his mark as a Broadway comedian, continued his career in movies when he signed with the Famous Players Film Company. Uncle Sidney Drew remarried after the death of his first wife, Gladys, and he and his new wife, Lucille, signed with Metro to write, direct, and star in more than 50 one-reel films, billed as Metro-Drew Comedies, in 1916. Sidney and Gladys's son, S. Rankin Drew, directed several highly praised movies before he met an early death as a volunteer fighting for the Allies in World War I, which had broken out in August 1914.

Although the United States did not enter the European conflict until 1917, Ethel Barrymore was more aware of the war's progress than most Americans. Her friends in England, with whom she still corresponded regularly, had husbands, fathers, sons, and other relatives directly involved in the fighting. She read each published casualty list with particular dread. Of more immediate concern, her husband, Russell Colt, went to Europe shortly after the war began to volunteer as an ambulance driver in France. He returned unharmed just before America declared war on Germany, then went into officers' training and was commissioned in the U.S. Army. Jack Barrymore tried to enlist in the American Expeditionary Force but, fortunately for Ethel's peace of mind, did not meet the physical requirements. Lionel Barrymore, who had already sustained a knee injury that would bother him for the rest of his life, was also ineligible for service.

Although the United States was not a combatant during the war's early years, most Americans had discontinued all unnecessary European travel. This included Ethel Barrymore, who was busy earning money and spending her limited free time with her children at the house in Mamaroneck, now a showplace of Westchester County. While fulfilling her contract with Metro, she continued to appear onstage, scoring another triumph in *The Shadow*, originally slated to be performed in Paris but acquired by Charles Frohman when the war made its presentation impossible in France. Frohman continued to have crucial business dealings in London and felt his annual trips were essential, even though sea journeys had become increasingly dangerous because of German submarines cruising the Atlantic. Despite a warning to travelers published in April 1914 by the German embassy, he sailed to England on the *Lusitania* on May 1, 1915. A German torpedo hit the ship 6 days later, and Frohman was among the 1,195 lost when the liner went down.

In May 1914, Barrymore joined her uncle John Drew onstage for the first time in 18 years in A Scrap of Paper. *She admired his acting prowess, urbanity, and mischievous sense of humor; he took great pride in the success of his niece's career.*

The marriage of Ethel Barrymore and Russell Colt was not a happy one, but Barrymore sincerely wanted to make it a success. Despite Colt's frequent and lengthy trips to Palm Beach, Florida, the couple appeared together socially as often as possible and steadfastly denied rumors of discord.

Barrymore was in Boston when news of the *Lusitania* disaster and the death of Charles Frohman was confirmed. The tragedy affected her more deeply than any other during the war. Charles Frohman had worked with Mum Mum, with John Drew, and with Lionel and Jack Barrymore. He had given Ethel her first roles and helped her to make the difficult transition from ingenue to dramatic actress. No one could ever take Frohman's place in Barrymore's career or in her heart, but his role as manager and agent for the family was assumed by Alf Hayman, the new head of Frohman Enterprises.

By the end of the war, Barrymore was widely hailed as the "first actress of our stage" and was also known and loved for her work in vaudeville and in the movies, which continued when she contracted with Metro in 1917 for five additional pictures. During the summer of 1918, while Barrymore was at Mamaroneck with her children, Alf Hayman called one day to say he had "something wonderful" for her. It turned out to be the first two acts of a new play by Zoe Akins, titled *Déclassée*. The piece was unfinished, but Hayman predicted it would be the greatest play yet for Barrymore. She was entranced with the partial script and pleaded with Hayman, "Please make sure that nothing happens to interfere with my getting this play." But events were about to occur that would put both the production and Barrymore's role in *Déclassée* in jeopardy.

A telegram from the Actors' Equity Association informed her that a strike was being called against all of New York City's producers. Zoe Akins had finished the play, and Barrymore was looking forward to starting rehearsals. At first that seemed far more important to Barrymore than the impending strike. Her uncle John Drew sat her down to explain that actors were seeking better contracts, better working conditions, and reduction of the non-paying rehearsal period. He convinced her that major stars such as he and Barrymore had to lend their support for the strike to succeed.

After talking to Drew, Barrymore rallied to the cause and wrote a letter to the association that read, in part: "While my entire theatrical career has been associated with but one management, from which I have received only fairness and consideration, I feel the traditions of my family and my personal predilections ally me logically and irremediably with the members of my profession in the Actors' Equity Association."

The strike was called in August 1919, and in its support Barrymore put her career on the line for her fellow performers. She refused to take part in the rehearsals for *Déclassée*, provided direct financial aid for the strikers, made public appearances, and gathered the family, both Drews and Barrymores, to back Actors' Equity. The efforts were successful; and in honor of her contribution Barrymore was appointed as a member of the group that signed a new five-year labor pact between actors and management. Her good friend Augustus Thomas presided over the ceremony and Arthur Hopkins, another close friend, served as spokesman for the managers. Hayman, unhappy over the delays in the production of *Déclassée*, was glad to finally get the rehearsals under way. His behavior toward Barrymore after the strike and his obvious dissatisfaction with her actions during it resulted in her eventual departure from Frohman Enterprises.

Déclassée was among Barrymore's greatest hits, running at the Empire Theatre for more than 200 performances and breaking all the Empire's box office records. The following year Barrymore took the play on tour with equal success. In it she portrayed a titled English lady who is stripped of her social standing after being unfaithful to her husband. The role gave her an opportunity to display tremendous emotional range onstage.

During the tour Barrymore faced her first serious illness. Afflicted with a sudden, excruciating pain just before her death scene in the play, she had to be carried back onstage and placed on a sofa to complete her performance. When the final curtain fell, Barrymore collapsed. She was rushed to a hospital in Cincinnati and diagnosed as having a crippling form of arthritis. Later, after she returned to New York and entered Flower Hospital, the doctors concluded that she was suffering from a streptococcic infection of the tonsils. A tonsillectomy and several weeks of recuperation in the hospital took care of the problem.

During this period Barrymore sought and received permission from the Catholic church to divorce Russell Colt—on the condition that she never remarry. Colt had been openly involved in a romance with a young, wealthy, married socialite—a public scandal that Barrymore could not tolerate. The Colts were legally separated on the day she left Flower Hospital, and two years later, in 1923, their divorce was final. She would later write, "My career, instead of interfering with my marriage, helped to make it possible, and helped me to keep on trying as long and as determinedly as I did, to save it." Russell Colt did not contest the divorce brought by his wife on the grounds of desertion and nonsupport. For the sake of the children, their relationship continued to be friendly. Weekly dinners at Mamaroneck were standard, and Colt was always welcome at Christmas, Easter, and other family gatherings.

The Colt children were raised in much the same manner as Ethel Barrymore and her brothers had been. Sammy attended a boarding school in Canterbury, Connecticut. Young Ethel was bundled off to the same convent in Philadelphia that Ethel Barrymore had attended. Jackie, the youngest, was enrolled in a boarding school near Mamaroneck. The two boys would later attend a series of the best and most expensive schools available. Their sister would graduate from the convent and then attend a private school in Verona, Italy, where she studied languages, art, and singing.

In the first half of the 1920s, Ethel Barrymore starred in a variety of plays.

Barrymore called her children "simply heaven, the most important thing in my life" and claimed, "More and more as things began to go wrong, or not so well, with my marriage, they were my happiness." Their grandfather Samuel Colt doted on them even after his son and Barrymore were divorced.

Her brother Jack directed her in *Clair de Lune*, written by his second wife, Michael Strange. Unfortunately, the critics disliked it intensely. Ethel Barrymore toured again with *Déclassée*, still a great success, and then appeared in *Rose Bernd*. That play's run ended rather quickly when, at the age of 43, Barrymore took on the role of Juliet in *Romeo and Juliet*. At the same time, Jane Cowl, a younger (and thinner) performer, appeared in the same role in a different production. Barrymore said of her *Romeo and Juliet*: "This was not a successful venture. The public didn't like the scenery—they didn't like the company—they didn't like me." She next appeared in a light comedy, *The Laughing Lady*, then took the stage for one week with her uncle John Drew in a classic production of Sheridan's *The School for Scandal*. *A Royal Fandango*, by the author of *Déclassée*, followed, along with several roles in Shakespearean productions. Some of these plays received less than rave reviews, and although Barrymore's celebrity status never waned, she began to search for a powerful dramatic role, something special to rekindle the adoration of her fans. Her greatest hit of the decade was Somerset Maugham's *The Constant Wife*, which ran from 1926 to 1929 and provided Barrymore with an excellent income. The play failed to give her the critical acclaim she wanted, but the audience loved it. Jack Barrymore, after seeing her performance in *The Constant Wife*, recalled telling his sister, "During the performance, I did not hear one person in the audience cough—a remarkable phenomenon."

She said, "But I don't let them cough."

"And how is that done?" asked Jack.

"I just turn on something inside myself," she replied, "and they don't dare cough."

Ethel Barrymore called her ability "the thing you must do to an audience," and claimed, "I was always enormously conscious of the audience." Theatergoers could sometimes be unruly, distracting, and exasperating. Occasionally Barrymore took more forceful action. Her nephew retold an old family story about Barrymore performing a scene with an elderly character actor, Charles Cherry, whose hearing was not what it had been. A group arrived late, noisily entered their stage box, and settled down to whispering and crinkling their programs. Barrymore stepped to the front of the stage and called up: "Excuse me, I can hear every word you're saying, but Mr. Cherry is slightly hard of hearing. I wonder if you would speak up for him?" The disturbance ceased.

In December 1928, Barrymore received the highest honor yet granted to an actress. The Shubert brothers, the most illustrious theatrical producers of that era, built a new theater on New York's West 47th Street and named it the Ethel Barrymore Theatre. Barrymore opened it by starring in a new production, *The Kingdom of God*, written by G. Martínez Sierra and produced by the Shuberts. Under the name E. M. Blyth, Barrymore directed the play, which consisted of three acts, each devoted to a stage in the life of a wellborn Spanish nun, and she considered her role and her direction a triumph. The public seemed to like it; the critics disagreed. Still, as Barrymore contemplated a theater bearing her name and looked back on her beginning as the young ingenue who suffered from terrible stage fright, she felt a remarkable sense of accomplishment. Always modest, though, she once said she wholeheartedly agreed with a writer who remarked she would have rather it had been named after John Drew.

Despite the constant public acclaim and the ensuing publicity, one aspect of Barrymore's life during this period remains a mystery: her romantic relationships. She confided to a friend: "It's not the church affiliation that prevents me from marrying again. The plain truth of the matter is that I've never met a man I would want to be married to." She did, in fact, remain single for the rest of her life.

The 1920s had been good to Barrymore, but the decade that followed did not start well. The stock market crash of October 1929 plunged America into the most severe economic depression in its history. Theater and vaudeville suffered diminishing box office receipts as audiences flocked to the less expensive movies, which now featured sound. As the 1930s began, Barrymore was spending most of her time onstage touring the vaudeville circuit with her old standby, *The Twelve Pound Look*, and wondering where her career would take her in the future. Her brothers had found acclaim in Hollywood, but her last picture, a silent movie, had been made in 1919. Always praised for her wonderful voice and speaking ability, she viewed the lucrative new "talkies," as movies with sound were called, with more than passing interest.

John met Ethel at the Pasadena, California, railroad station when she journeyed west in 1932 to start work on her first motion picture in 13 years—and the first one she ever made with sound. Ethel valued his advice about moviemaking, for he had become one of Hollywood's most popular stars after leaving the theater.

SEVEN

A Troubled Reign

"A very thin time" was Barrymore's description of the spring of 1932. Her theatrical fortunes had plunged along with the nation's economy, but out in California moviemakers were thriving. That year Irving Thalberg, whose brilliance had made him the 25-year-old head of production at Metro-Goldwyn-Mayer (MGM) in 1924, conceived of a blockbuster historical epic about the fall of the Russian ruling dynasty, entitled *Rasputin and the Empress*. He turned to America's own royal family of performers for his cast, and in June 1932, Ethel Barrymore joined her brothers in Hollywood to begin rehearsals. Lionel recalled: "Jack and I were both amazed and tickled pink and went about praising Thalberg's powers of persuasion. Privately we thought that it might not be unreasonable to assume that the lady had been to some extent influenced by one hundred thousand dollars."

The three were genuinely glad to see one another, however. As Ethel admitted, it was one of the very few times the siblings had spent time together since the long-ago days in Mum Mum's house in Philadelphia. Ethel was not used to moviemaking and admitted to needing some help adapting to the movies' new sound tracks—help that her brothers happily provided. The studio's publicists seized upon the idea of sibling rivalry as a way to attract attention to the movie and began printing exaggerated stories of fights between the three Barrymores. When Ethel arrived in California, one reporter asked if she was concerned about appearing on screen with such experienced scene stealers as her brothers.

Jack, who had come to the train station to welcome his sister, replied glibly: "You need not worry about Miss Barrymore getting nervous. She'll be standing right before the camera—in

81

front of us." Jack was well known for his quick way with words, women, and whiskey bottles, and the quip was meant lightheartedly. When Ethel got off the train at Pasadena, he did her a great favor by whispering in her ear, "For God's sake, get Bill Daniels." Daniels was a cameraman whose artful work had disguised the effects of some of Jack's more punishing binges, and one star, Greta Garbo, absolutely refused to work in a film without him. Ethel did appear at her best as the empress, thanks in part to heeding Jack's admonition.

She held up her end of the teasing as well. She later commented, in response to a question regarding her brothers' acting, "Lionel is the best character actor in the world, and I love John when he isn't *profiling himself* through a role—handsome though his profile may be."

With rumors of sibling rivalry racing through Hollywood, MGM warned the public to look for real fireworks when filming began. The gossip about the feuding Barrymores increased until Hollywood wits referred to the picture as *Disputin' and the Empress*. The Barrymores denied all the stories. Time and distance had done nothing to weaken the bonds forged in childhood.

Left to right: *Lionel, Ethel, and John in California in 1932. When the three Barrymores worked together on* Rasputin and the Empress *for Metro-Goldwyn-Mayer, the studio's publicists churned out scandalous, but wholly fabricated, stories of sibling rivalry.*

When a photographer asked Jack to tell his sister something, Jack offered: *"Tell her something! I should say not. But I will ask her something."* Despite all the stories of feuds and fights, the Barrymores enjoyed their time together and often gathered at the enormous home Ethel had rented. By then there was quite a clan, including Ethel's three children, Jack's third wife, Dolores, and their two children, and Lionel's second wife, Irene, whom Ethel did not particularly like but was gracious to nonetheless. The filming of the picture was the last time all 10 were together.

Ethel Barrymore had only eight weeks between theater engagements to finish the movie. Several important scenes were not yet complete when she had to leave Hollywood, and they were dropped from the script. The time constraints and hastily composed script irritated Ethel. She described the disorder: "It was maddening, to say the least. I'd be handed several lines to say on a sheet of paper, without knowing what relation they had to other parts of the film, and then when I arrived on the set, I'd be told that the dialogue had to be revised. When I read this, it bore no connection with the preceding text." Having spent years learning a variety of long, demanding parts, she was able to deal with the situation but was not above a display of temper. Given an hour to learn three pages of dialogue, she retorted, "You must want me to recite it backwards."

Though the trade papers undoubt-edly exaggerated the intrafamilial tension, the trio certainly pulled more than a few tricks on each other. One recorded exchange ran as follows:

Lionel growled at Jack, "Great stuff, kid. If you want the whole camera, say so," as he moved to reveal exactly half of his brother to the cameraman.

Shoving Lionel farther to center stage, Jack replied, "Don't pull any of your scene-stealing tricks on me, old man."

"If you two want the whole camera, I still have a voice, you know," Ethel boomed.

The convergence of Barrymores, which Douglas Fairbanks compared to "trying out airplane motors in a drawing room," turned out to be the least of MGM's problems with the picture. The contents of the script proved more troubling. The *New York Herald Tribune* reviewer wrote of *Rasputin and the Empress*: "It achieves one feat which is not inconsiderable. It manages to libel even the despised Rasputin." Jack had played Rasputin's killer, a character based on Prince Felix Youssoupoff. The prince's wife, Irina Alexandrovna, claimed that a character called Natasha was based on her and portrayed her libelously. The couple sued the studio in New York and London, and the reputed cost to MGM of the out-of-court settlement exceeded $1 million, an enormous sum in the 1930s. The affair led to the introduction of a line that preceded every subsequent Hollywood movie: "The events and characters in this film are fictional and any resemblance to persons living or dead is purely coincidental."

Ethel Barrymore missed the premiere of the movie, for she had returned to the East, begun rehearsals, and gone on tour with her next play, *Encore* (retitled *An Amazing Career*), by the time the movie opened. She seemed not to have been particularly reluctant to leave the studios behind. When asked about Hollywood on the train trip back east to New York, Barrymore replied, "Hollywood is a factory. My brothers have become institutionalized factory hands. I could not." She later gave another impression of Hollywood: "The people are unreal. The flowers are unreal. They don't smell. The fruit is unreal. It doesn't taste of anything. The whole place is a *set*, a glaring, gaudy, nightmarish set, built up in the desert."

Although the movie opened to mixed reviews, the Barrymore family's acting was appraised in glowing terms. The picture remains the only recorded instance of the three siblings acting together and provides an opportunity to see Ethel Barrymore in her prime, for she did not return to Hollywood until more than a decade later.

"The next year [1933] was a very bad and harrowing time," Barrymore stated. It was the year that President Roosevelt ordered all the banks closed for a day, and it "was the only year after I first went on stage when I was not at work," Barrymore admitted. The nation was in the iron grip of the Great Depression. Barrymore had two consecutive failures onstage and retreated with her children, now fully grown, to Mamaroneck. Her future, and theirs, now seemed in serious doubt. Thus far, Barrymore had overcome every obstacle on her path to stardom, and she had made a fortune along the way. But now that she was in her fifties and competing for each role with newer and younger performers, such as Katharine Cornell, Helen Hayes, Tallulah Bankhead, and Gertrude Lawrence, it looked as though her days as a star might be over. To make matters worse, her money was gone. She had spent it lavishly when she had it, not on jewels, furs, or automobiles, but on living well—traveling and dining in style, always with her friends and family—and had devoted generous amounts to her children's education. Never having invested, she had built up no capital or savings. In an effort to pay her pressing bills, Barrymore took the tried-and-true *Twelve Pound Look* to England, where it failed miserably. Her creditors renewed their attacks, and life seemed bitter for the great lady.

Many years later, when a reporter asked, "How did you handle all that?" she replied, in part: "When life knocks you to your knees, which it always does and always will—well, that's the best position in which to pray, isn't it? On your knees." She also said, "You must learn day by day, year by year, to broaden your horizon. The more things you love, the more you are interested in, the more you enjoy, the more you are indignant about—the more you have left when anything happens." She attended every game of the 1936 World Series and continued to patronize the boxing matches in Madison Square Garden as well as a variety of recitals, symphonies, and concerts.

Between 1930 and 1937, Barrymore appeared on Broadway only once, when she was invited by Eva Le Gallienne to be a guest star in a play called *L'Aiglon*. Midway through the decade she gave some readings from *The Kingdom of God* on radio, using her unforgettable voice to its best effect. This led to several appearances on "Radio Theatre of the Air." In 1936 she once again took *The Constant Wife* on tour, but it barely made expenses. At the beginning of 1937 the Internal Revenue Service sued Barrymore for nearly $100,000 in back taxes and interest owed from 1921 to 1929. She could only pay $7,500, and the IRS accepted it, recording that "at the present time there is practically no demand for her services. And she has no future on the stage." Ethel Barrymore reluctantly concluded that her life in the theater was over, and she decided to retire from public life. She made the announcement on a radio program while she and guests were playing a popular game called Knock-Knock.

When Barrymore's turn came she

Stephen Haggard (left) appeared in 1938 with Barrymore in Whiteoaks. *She used a minimum of makeup and all her talent to create her critically acclaimed portrayal of an ancient matriarch.*

said, "This is my last public appearance and I will now devote my life to teaching the art of acting." Turning to the commentator, she said, "Knock-Knock."

"Who's there?" came the standard response.

"Saul."

"Saul who?"

"Saul there is—there isn't any more," she said, referring to her often-quoted and mimicked line from the long-ago play *Sunday*.

Barrymore never did launch her teaching career, although her long service onstage provided her with many insights useful to young performers. About working in plays written by great dramatists, she said: "Always I have tried to leave my authors alone. You don't have to be bewildered by Shakespeare. There he is. Leave him alone. Say what he says and thank God that he has given you a trumpet through which to blow so sweetly. You don't have to be bewildered by Ibsen. There he is. Leave him alone, and he will tell a woman's life in three hours." Playing in a light comedy presented a different set of problems. She claimed: "A light comedy is the most tiring of all to play, the most difficult to keep up. You are taking the part of a person who is just like everyone in the audience. And the fact that you have to be natural is much harder than doing emotional parts. People don't realize this. It is much more difficult to be convincing in a modern comedy when every woman in the audience thinks she is

more or less like the woman you are playing."

Instead of starting an acting academy, that October she began a 26-week radio series featuring 30-minute episodes of her greatest plays, given in chronological order. She began with *Captain Jinks of the Horse Marines*. By the end of 1937 she had settled with the IRS, paid off her most persistent creditors, and had her finances back in order. At last, she returned to the stage.

In *The Ghost of Yankee Doodle*, Sidney Howard's play about the dangerous growth of fascism, Barrymore played a gracious lady who presides over her family's political squabbles. The play was received with tepid enthusiasm, but Barrymore got raves. Her nephew John Drew Devereaux had the role of her son in the production, and he later spoke of his impressions of his imposing aunt. "She seemed to have, as I suppose all great stage stars do, at least five different points of concentration. She could be playing a scene with you and seemingly looking right into the innermost depths of your eyes, but if somebody moved over on the other side of the stage she would notice it immediately." True to the Drew-Barrymore tradition, she watched over her young relative. When another actress said her line so quickly that there was no time for the audience to laugh at a line John Drew Devereaux had just spoken, he recalled that "all of a sudden everything seemed to stop in time." Barrymore froze the offender with a look of rage and told her, "Don't you ever do that again!" right onstage. She did not speak to the actress for the rest of the play's run.

Her family helped her out as well. When Lionel was passing through New York, he stopped by to tell her about a play he had seen in London, called *Whiteoaks*, which featured a part he considered suitable for Ethel. The role was that of a 102-year-old matriarch, and when Ethel was asked how she felt about playing so old a character, she replied, "Perfectly delighted. That's just what I feel." Her portrayal was impressive enough to keep the play on Broadway for the remainder of the season.

In August 1939, Barrymore turned 60, and a few short weeks later she heard on the radio that England was again at war. Although she had a son in uniform, Barrymore did not suffer a tragic personal loss, as she had with Charles Frohman's death during World War I.

She returned to work, playing a 97-year-old South African woman in *Farm of Three Echoes*. A psychiatrist sent her a letter, praising her work as "the most magnificent portrayal of senility" he had ever seen. The critics were equally pleased with Barrymore's performance but gave the play poor marks.

As the decade closed, Barrymore continued to search for a particular play—one with a powerful role that could again catapult her back into the stellar realm she had known so well.

The Corn Is Green *marked Barrymore's return as an undisputed star.*
The play opened in New York in 1942 and ran for two years on tour.

EIGHT

Curtain Call

In 1940, Herman Shumlin, a theatrical producer, telephoned Barrymore to tell her he had purchased the rights to an English play titled *The Corn Is Green*. He told her it was a simple piece about an elderly Englishwoman with a gift for teaching and asked if she would like to read it. Barrymore, who had despaired of finding a vehicle suited to an aging actress, agreed at once.

She later recalled in her memoirs: "The play and I were instant and terrific successes and, believe me, it was high time for the success. It came at a crucial moment in my life and made all the difference."

Barrymore, clad in a plain shirtwaist, skirt, and straw hat, rode a bicycle onto the stage of the National Theatre on November 26, 1940, to begin the play's New York run. She scored a triumph with audiences and critics alike and spent the next three years, one in New York and two on tour, starring in *The Corn Is Green*. It would be—along with *Déclassée*, *The Constant Wife*, and *The Twelve Pound Look*—one of her favorite plays. She had a packed house every night and a contract that rewarded her for the crowds she drew—she received $1,000 a week in salary and 7 percent of the gross ticket receipts.

Barrymore had more to celebrate than a successful play. February 4, 1941, marked the 40th anniversary of Barrymore's first starring appearance onstage, in *Captain Jinks of the Horse Marines*. To commemorate this milestone, the NBC Radio Network presented a half-hour program as a tribute to Barrymore's career from *Captain Jinks* to *The Corn Is Green*. Among the many notables paying homage were her two brothers, Lionel and Jack Barrymore. This was the first time all three Barrymores appeared on the same radio program. Lionel later recorded in his own autobiography, *We Barrymores*, how he teased Jack and praised his sister on the air. Jack saluted his sister's "gaiety, charm and splendor. One has only to think of her to be invested with a God-given quality of humility."

The tributes were sometimes sentimental, but Barrymore had not grown softhearted in her later years. Remembering the bleak days of the previous decade when she had had so much difficulty finding a good part, in private she remarked astringently: "Now that I'm in a hit people I haven't seen or heard from in years are banging at my door. They're crawling out from under rocks and worming their way out of the woodwork. What scum!"

Sincere accolades continued to come her way. In May the nation's first lady, Eleanor Roosevelt, presented Barrymore with the Barter Theatre Award "for the outstanding performance given by an American actress during the current theater season." Mrs. Roosevelt claimed, "Miss Barrymore is one of the first people who made me love the theater."

While Barrymore toured with *The Corn Is Green*, RKO, a leading studio, sent an emissary to talk to her about playing the role of Ma Mott in the movie version of a novel entitled *None But the Lonely Heart*, in which Cary

Cary Grant costarred with Barrymore in None But the Lonely Heart, *her first film in 12 years. Absence from the silver screen had not rusted her skills; her performance won her the Academy Award for best supporting actress in 1944.*

Lionel (left) and John (right) each present an apple to John's daughter Diana after all three appeared on a radio program on March 6, 1942. According to Drew-Barrymore tradition, older family members awarded an apple to a young relative for a particularly good debut. A sadder legacy also haunted Diana; fewer than three months after the photograph was taken, John died from the effects of alcoholism, and Diana succumbed to the same disease in 1960.

Grant would costar as her son. Barrymore agreed to do the movie only after RKO made a deal with Herman Shumlin to pay the salaries of the cast and crew of *The Corn Is Green* during her absence from the production and to recompense Shumlin and all the theaters that would lose her services while she made the picture. It was an expensive proposition, but the studio executives thought Barrymore was worth it.

Twelve years had passed since her last movie. Barrymore performed superbly during the rehearsals, but during the actual takes she became extremely nervous. Apparently, after four decades onstage, then on radio, and finally on screen, her old stage fright could still plague her. Clifford Odets, the director and screenwriter, told Cary Grant that he planned to film Barrymore during what she thought were rehearsals. Odets's ruse worked magnificently, and soon Barrymore's confidence had grown so much that she abandoned the scheme. Barrymore was pleased with her work on the movie, but her heart remained in the theater. She happily noted in her autobiography that when the picture finished at noon one day she was able to catch the Santa Fe Chief to New York an hour later to resume her tour of *The Corn Is Green*. She was even happier when she won the 1944 Academy Award for best performance by an actress in a supporting role.

While Ethel Barrymore reached a new peak of fame, her brother Jack was in a slow but tragic decline. Of the three Barrymore children, he had been closest to his father just before Maurice's health deteriorated. For years afterward Jack was tormented by nightmares of dying the way Maurice Barrymore had, but the nightmares did not stop him from drinking as heavily as his father. He had been treated during the 1930s for alcoholism, and the illness caused temporary losses of memory along with a liver ailment. Although Jack also had severe headaches and an ulcer, he refused to stop drinking. Ethel and Lionel knew that their brother was killing himself. Tragically, they were unable to get him to stop.

On May 19, 1942, Jack collapsed in a dressing room after rehearsing a radio show. The doctors said that Barrymore was suffering from bronchial pneumonia complicated by liver and kidney failure. Lionel and several of Jack's close friends kept vigil at the hospital; Ethel was constantly informed of Jack's condition, but at his request, she stayed on the road with *The Corn Is Green*. For the next few days Jack Barrymore lapsed into an intermittent coma. He was often heard to mumble, "Mum Mum." He died on the night of May 29, 1942, ringing down the final curtain on a magnificent stage, screen, and radio career.

The two surviving Barrymores, Ethel and Lionel, were also plagued by illness during the next few years. Lionel suffered from such severe arthritis that he was forced to use a wheelchair fulltime. During the winter of 1944–45, while Ethel played on Broadway in *Embezzled Heaven*, she contracted pneumonia and had to be hospitalized. A succession of severe colds followed. She recalled the bright, warm sunlight of California and often thought of the last days her mother, Georgie Barrymore, spent in Santa Barbara. Late in 1945, Barrymore moved permanently to California to make movies. She wrote, "I had given fifty years to the theater and felt that I had done my bit, and besides, lately, in the theater in New York, I had come to feel a little as if I were Ruth amid the alien corn. And incidentally, in all the years I have never ceased to miss Mr. Frohman."

Following Barrymore's Academy Award, offers to appear in movies poured in. Her price was $100,000 per picture for what she deemed not particularly strenuous work. She once commented, "It's a shame to take their money. You work about two minutes, then go to your dressing room and read a detective story or listen to a ball game." Still, her work remained excellent, and she received another Academy Award nomination for her role in a 1946 murder mystery called *The Spiral Staircase*, in which she played a bedridden, elderly woman. A reviewer from *Time* magazine reported: "She spends most of this one propped up in bed, alternately purring and bellowing in a voice not unlike brother Lionel's. She is superbly effective."

At the age of 67, Barrymore was far from bedridden herself. During the next 5 years she made 16 movies. Director George Cukor claimed: "Why if Ethel's talking to a football player, she knows as much about the subject as he does.

Or baseball—the stagehands used to keep track of the scores by listening at her dressing-room door. And politics. . . . She simply doesn't think old, talk old, or feel old." As in her youth, she was still a voracious reader. Her son Sammy Colt had returned from the service at the end of World War II and had chosen to work in public relations in California to be near his mother. They bought a home on the Palos Verdes peninsula with a magnificent view of the Pacific, 20 miles down the coast from Hollywood. The house was soon jammed with books that Ethel considered treasures. They spilled out of bookshelves, covered the tabletops, and overflowed into the garage. Eventually, Sammy had to complain that there was no room to park his car.

Barrymore's youth had been filled with gracious parties and sparkling conversation, and she continued her love of creative society in her later years. At her Palos Verdes home she regally presided over dinner parties at the head of a huge mahogany table. Her guests were a varied and distinguished lot. The usually reclusive Greta Garbo was happy to attend a dinner with several acting colleagues, including Billie Burke, who played the good witch in *The Wizard of Oz*; Garbo was reported to have laughed heartily at one point, a rare occurrence. Writers such as Somerset Maugham, composers such as Irving Berlin and Cole Porter, musicians such as the pianists Arthur Rubinstein and Vladimir Horowitz, and old friends such as Elsie De Wolfe and Zoe Akins—all eagerly accepted Barry-

Barrymore holds one of her grandchildren, John Drew Miglietta. Although she gave her Mamaroneck, New York, home to her daughter, Ethel Colt Miglietta, after moving permanently to California, she often returned east for visits.

more's invitations. Active in politics as well, Barrymore became an ardent Democrat and once snubbed Richard M. Nixon at a party.

On her 70th birthday Hollywood paid Barrymore an unprecedented honor. The Motion Picture Academy joined with NBC radio to present a show heard worldwide featuring 50 celebrities paying homage—through prerecorded messages—to "the queen of the theater's royal family." Jack Barrymore was gone, but his voice was heard on the show, thanks to a recording made in the 1941 radio salute to Barrymore. It brought tears to many eyes, including Ethel's. Others paying their respects included Alfred Lunt, Lynn Fontanne, Spencer Tracy, Cary Grant, Katharine Cornell, Herbert Hoover, Eleanor Roosevelt, and President Harry Truman. Barrymore also received a congratulatory telegram from England, simply signed "Winston," from her old friend Winston Churchill.

Barrymore had given the Mamaroneck house to her daughter, now Ethel Colt Miglietta, who had become a singer and appeared with several opera companies. Barrymore traveled east less frequently, but she doted on her grandchildren and loved being called Mum Mum by this latest generation. She continued to work, claiming she needed the money, and made two movies in 1952 and two more in 1953. Never having received a high school diploma, she was greatly honored when New York University awarded her an honorary doctorate of fine arts in June

1952. During the next few years, she settled into semiretirement and withdrew to her gardens, where she grew, in great profusion, those California flowers that she had once complained looked "unreal."

In November 1955, Lionel Barrymore, who had been restricted to a wheelchair for several years, was involved in an automobile accident. Although not seriously injured, he had an existing heart condition that was complicated by the accident. He died on November 15 and was buried at Calvary Cemetery, in a crypt above his brother Jack's.

Ethel Barrymore had begun writing her memoirs before Lionel's death. In an interview with Howard Thompson of the *New York Times*, she reported that her book was being written in her own hand, pointing out acidly that "Lionel's was *ghosted*, of course." She sold the serial rights of her book to the *Ladies' Home Journal*, and when Lionel died just before excerpts were to appear, the magazine's editor called to ask if Barrymore wanted to include a final word about her brother. She wrote: "Since I have finished this book, Lionel has died. I would like to think he and Jack are together—and that they will be glad to see me. E.B."

Memories was published in 1955. Friends were congratulatory, but a few voiced disappointment over some glaring omissions in Barrymore's writing about her and her family's personal life. Also, Barrymore had not been noted for her record keeping. She had grandly announced, before publication, that she would write her memoirs "without dates and things like that."

The book brought some additional celebrity and a round of television appearances. Barrymore had appeared in a one-act Tennessee Williams play in 1953 and had hosted a show called "The Ethel Barrymore Theater" for a short period in 1954. Despite describing live television as "a killer" and the new medium as "hell" to work in, she agreed to be a guest performer in several dramatic productions of "The General Electric Theater" and "Playhouse 90." She had never sat through *Rasputin and the Empress* in a movie theater and, for the first time, saw the picture on television. Age had not dimmed her wit, as was evident when she wrote about the film, "I thought *I* was pretty good, but what those *two boys* were up to I'll never know."

As Barrymore grew older, she spent more and more time at home and was often restricted to bed. She had lots of visitors, many of whom commented that Barrymore's beauty was still evident and that she remained active and alert. One male friend, pausing at the door of her bedroom before entering for a visit, asked, "May I see the most beautiful woman in California?" Barrymore's still-resonant voice rumbled back: "And *why* have I been demoted?" Katharine Hepburn, who enjoyed dropping in often, said: "She has more friends than anyone I know, but she's not a dear gentle soul. Barrymores don't come like that. She has a trenchant

wit. . . . She makes appallingly accurate observations."

As the summer of 1959 began, Barrymore's health took a turn for the worse. On June 17, a Wednesday night, she stayed up to listen to a baseball doubleheader between the Los Angeles Dodgers and the Milwaukee Braves. The next morning she awoke briefly and asked her nurse, "Is everybody happy? I want everybody to be happy. I know I'm happy," then went back to sleep. She did not wake up again, and that night the lights of the Ethel Barrymore Theatre were dimmed for five minutes in her memory.

Although Lionel, Jack, and Ethel were gone, the entertainment world was not bereft of members of the Drew-Barrymore clan. Many sought careers in films and on the stage. Some met disappointing failures; others scored successes. John Drew Devereaux, who had been privileged to perform with Ethel in *The Ghost of Yankee Doodle*, spent many years in the theater and then became a stage manager on Broadway. One of Jack Barrymore's grandchildren, Drew Barrymore, starred in *E.T.* and *Poltergeist* before beginning a valiant battle with alcohol and drug addiction, an unfortunate legacy from her grandfather.

Ethel Barrymore's triumphs were evanescent—each time the curtain came down, her performance was lost to posterity. She was at her best before the footlights and an audience, in a medium that later generations can never fully appreciate. In a television tribute presented a few months before her death, actor and director Orson Welles attempted to illuminate her achievements for those who had never seen her. His comments summed up a glittering age and a brilliant career: "Nowadays, my dear great-grandchildren, we are so used to flooding our parlors with entertainment by just turning on a sort of faucet, that you may not find it easy to imagine that olden time when to see a play people actually went to a theater, and got themselves all dressed up to do it. A play was an occasion, a gala event. Gilded and gay, with its crimson hangings and its crystal chandeliers, the theater was nothing so much as a ballroom, and attending it was like visiting a royal palace. Well, my dear great-grandchildren, in those olden days, in that enchanted kingdom called the Theater, there reigned a great queen: Miss Ethel Barrymore."

Surrounded by admirers and showered with honors during her last years, Barrymore attended a dinner party staged by MGM for her 70th birthday. The star-studded gathering included (front row, left to right) Lionel Barrymore, Ethel, Spencer Tracy, and George Cukor; (back row, left to right) Billie Burke, Judy Garland, Lucille Watson, Katharine Hepburn, Constance Collier, and Laura Healy.

CHRONOLOGICAL LISTING OF FILMS

1914   *The Nightingale.* All Star Feature Corporation. Directed by Augustus Thomas.

1915   *The Final Judgment.* Metro Pictures Corporation. Directed by Edwin Carewe.

1916   *The Kiss of Hate.* Columbia-Metro. Directed by William Nigh.
        The Awakening of Helen Ritchie. Metro-Rolfe. Directed by John W. Noble.

1917   *The White Raven.* Metro-Rolfe. Directed by George D. Baker.
        The Call of Her People. Metro-Rolfe. Directed by John W. Noble.
        The Greatest Power. Metro-Rolfe. Directed by Edwin Carewe.
        The Lifted Veil. Metro-Rolfe. Directed by George D. Baker.
        Life's Whirlpool. Metro-Rolfe. Directed by Lionel Barrymore.
        The Eternal Mother. Metro-Rolfe. Directed by Frank Reicher.
        An American Widow. Metro-Rolfe. Directed by Frank Reicher.

1918   *Our Mrs. McChesney.* Metro-Rolfe. Directed by Ralph W. Ince. (Based on the stage play of the same name.)
        The Divorcee. Metro-Rolfe. Directed by Herbert Blache. (Based on the stage play *Lady Frederick.*)

1932   *Rasputin and the Empress.* Metro-Goldwyn-Mayer. Directed by Richard Boleslawski and Charles Brabin.

1944   *None But the Lonely Heart.* RKO. Directed by Clifford Odets.

1946   *The Spiral Staircase.* RKO. Directed by Robert Siodmak.

1947   *The Farmer's Daughter.* RKO. Directed by H. C. Potter.
        Moss Rose. Twentieth Century-Fox. Directed by Gregory Ratoff.
        Night Song. RKO. Directed by John Cromwell.

1948   *The Paradine Case.* Selznick Releasing Organization. Directed by Alfred Hitchcock.
        Moonrise. Republic. Directed by Frank Borzage.
        Portrait of Jennie. Selznick Releasing Organization. Directed by William Dieterle.

1949   *The Great Sinner.* Metro-Goldwyn-Mayer. Directed by Robert Siodmak.
        That Midnight Kiss. Metro-Goldwyn-Mayer. Directed by Norman Taurog.
        The Red Danube. Metro-Goldwyn-Mayer. Directed by George Sidney.
        Pinky. Twentieth Century-Fox. Directed by Elia Kazan.

1951   *Kind Lady.* Metro-Goldwyn-Mayer. Directed by John Sturges.
        Daphne, The Virgin of the Golden Laurels. Metro-Goldwyn-Mayer. Narrated by Ethel Barrymore and Maurice Evans.
        The Secret of Convict Lake. Twentieth Century-Fox. Directed by Michael Gordon.
        It's a Big Country. Metro-Goldwyn-Mayer. Directed by Richard Thorpe, John Sturges, Charles Vidor, Don Weis, Clarence Brown, William A. Wellman, and Don Hartman.

1952   *Deadline, USA.* Twentieth Century-Fox. Directed by Richard Brooks.
        Just For You. Paramount. Directed by Elliott Nugent.

1953   *The Story of Three Loves.* Metro-Goldwyn-Mayer. Directed by Vincente Minnelli and Gottfried Reinhardt.
        Main Street to Broadway. Lester Cowan–Metro-Goldwyn-Mayer. Directed by Tay Garnett.

1954   *Young at Heart.* Warner Brothers. Directed by Gordon Douglas.

1957   *Johnny Trouble.* Clarion–Warner Brothers. Directed by John H. Auer.

FURTHER READING

Alpert, Hollis. *The Barrymores.* New York: Dial Press, 1964.

Barrymore, Ethel. *Memories.* New York: Harper & Brothers, 1955.

Barrymore, John. *Confessions of an Actor.* Indianapolis, IN: Bobbs-Merrill, 1926.

———. *We Three.* New York: Saalfield, 1935.

Barrymore, Lionel. *We Barrymores.* New York: Appleton-Century-Crofts, 1951.

Fowler, Gene. *Good Night, Sweet Prince.* New York: Viking Press, 1944.

Kotsilibas-Davis, James. *The Barrymores: The Royal Family in Hollywood.* New York: Crown, 1981.

———. *Great Times, Good Times: The Odyssey of Maurice Barrymore.* New York: Doubleday, 1977.

CHRONOLOGY

Aug. 15, 1879	Born Ethel Barrymore in Philadelphia
1886	Enters Convent of Notre Dame boarding school
1893	Mother, Georgie Drew Barrymore, dies
1894	Barrymore tours with her grandmother Louisa Lane Drew; makes stage debut in *The Rivals* in Montreal, Canada
1897	Louisa Lane Drew dies
1901	Barrymore stars in first Broadway play, *Captain Jinks of the Horse Marines*
1905	Father, Maurice Barrymore, dies
1909	Barrymore marries Russell Colt; gives birth to first child, Samuel Colt
1912	Gives birth to Ethel Barrymore Colt
1913	Gives birth to John Drew Colt
1915	Signs contract to appear in silent films; starts accepting leading roles in a variety of Broadway productions
1919	Stars in *Déclassée* on Broadway and on tour
1923	Divorces Russell Colt
1926	Begins starring in *The Constant Wife* on Broadway and on tour
1932	Costars in the film *Rasputin and the Empress* with brothers, Lionel and John
1937	Settles with Internal Revenue Service for payment of back taxes; appears on "Radio Theatre of the Air"
1940	Returns to Broadway as star of *The Corn Is Green*; tours for two years
1944	Wins Academy Award for performance in the film *None But the Lonely Heart*
1945	Moves to California with the intention of appearing exclusively in films
1949	NBC radio network celebrates Barrymore's 70th birthday with a tribute program
1955	Barrymore publishes her autobiography, *Memories*
1957	Makes last film appearance in *Johnny Trouble*
June 18, 1959	Dies at home in California

INDEX

PICTURE CREDITS

Alex Thorleifson, a free-lance writer and sculptor, was born and raised in Philadelphia, Pennsylvania. She and her husband, Bill, reside in Irvine, California, and have two children. Ms. Thorleifson attended the University of Pennsylvania and Orange Coast College where she won the Writer of the Year scholarship in 1985. She is a member of the South Coast Writer's Workshop for novelists and screenwriters and is the coauthor of *John Wayne—My Life with Duke*, with Pilar Wayne, published in 1987 by McGraw-Hill; and *Behind the Candelabra—My Life with Liberace*, with Scott Thorson, published in 1988 by E. P. Dutton. Her first novel, *Gallery*, was published in 1990 by Bantam Books.

Matina S. Horner is president emerita of Radcliffe College and associate professor of psychology and social relations at Harvard University. She is best known for her studies of women's motivation, achievement, and personality development. Dr. Horner serves on several national boards and advisory councils, including those of the National Science Foundation, Time Inc., and the Women's Research and Education Institute. She earned her B.A. from Bryn Mawr College and Ph.D. from the University of Michigan, and holds honorary degrees from many colleges and universities, including Mount Holyoke, Smith, Tufts, and the University of Pennsylvania.